"Julia Higgins is a dear friend and a much-valued colleague at Southeastern Baptist Theological Seminary. She is an excellent scholar and superb classroom teacher. She is also a gifted writer, as this book clearly demonstrates. If you are looking for a book that will well equip women (and men!) to faithfully interpret and expound the inerrant Word of God, I strongly encourage you to consider this one. It will serve you well."

—**Daniel Akin**, president and professor of preaching and
theology, Southeastern Baptist Theological Seminary

"The sheer breadth and clarity of wisdom distilled in this book is impressive! Not only does Dr. Higgins survey the essential components of biblical interpretation, and trusted methods for expositional teaching, she does so with a Christ-centered hermeneutic. Scripture is clear: women have been given teaching gifts to be used for the edification of the church. Julia helps us understand how to encourage and equip the women in our churches to use those gifts in a way that is faithful to the testimony of Scripture. Julia's contribution to the saints in the pages of this book is both admirable and commendable. This work deserves wide readership and an easily accessible place on any church leader's bookshelf."

—**Matt Capps**, senior pastor, Fairview Baptist Church, Apex, NC

"*Empowered and Equipped* is a needed resource for developing doctrinally sound Bible teachers in the church. With great clarity and wisdom, Dr. Higgins provides a compelling approach for women desiring theological depth in their teaching. I highly recommend this resource for women preparing to teach the Bible."

—**Emily Dean**, assistant professor of ministry to women,
New Orleans Baptist Theological Seminary

"If you are serious about learning to teach the Bible, this is the book you need. Julia Higgins has written the most comprehensive, systematic, and accessible book I've seen on the topic. She steers her readers through each step needed to faithfully interpret, apply, and teach a passage. Not only will I use this book as I help others learn to teach, I will return to it again and again to sharpen my own skills and grow as a teacher of God's Word."

—**Courtney Doctor**, author and coordinator of women's initiatives, The Gospel Coalition

"This is the book I've been hoping someone would write—a solid resource for women who want to be equipped to examine, understand, and exposit the Bible faithfully and soundly."

—**Nancy Guthrie**, author and Bible teacher

"One of the great needs in the local church is equipping and providing opportunities for women to teach the Bible. In this book, Dr. Julia Higgins provides a theologically rich and practical resource to help address this problem. This book is not just for women who have the spiritual gift of teaching (though these women will certainly gain much from reading this book). Because of the commands of the Great Commission we are all responsible for teaching the Bible; therefore, this book will benefit anyone. As one who is committed to seeing women equipped to be disciples who make disciples, I recommend this book to anyone who wants to participate in God's redemptive work."

—**Lesley Hildreth**, women's discipleship director, The Summit Church

"Equipping women to teach God's word is not just a nice, hopeful aspiration. It's a necessity for multiplying disciples and helping women know deeply about the God who reveals himself through Scripture and his redemptive plan for all people. I'm grateful Dr. Julia Higgins has compiled a resource that should be in every teacher's library. With this book, women will be challenged and encouraged to make Scripture come alive and transformational to those they teach."

—**Kelly King**, manager of magazines/devotional publishing and women's ministry training, Lifeway Christian Resources

"For anyone who wants to be equipped to teach the Bible, look no further than *Empowered and Equipped: Bible Exposition for Women Who Teach the Scriptures* by Julia Higgins. This book is a well-organized, insightful, practical, and beneficial guide for teaching God's Word with accuracy, clarity, and insight. I highly recommend this excellent resource!"

—**Melissa Kruger**, author and director of women's initiatives, The Gospel Coalition

"For years, many of us in the evangelical community have toed the line regarding the biblical guidelines for women to teach Scripture to other women and children, but not to men. Yet, simultaneous with this rigorous restriction has been our massive failure to provide opportunities and resources for God-called and Spirit-gifted women to carry out their task. My friend and co-laborer, Julia Higgins, has responded to the void. *Empowered and Equipped* not only celebrates the call and responsibility of female Bible teachers, but it also prepares them to do it. And Julia's commitment to solid biblical exposition further strengthens this book to be a critical tool for mentors, disciple-makers, churches, and ministry training schools to mobilize a generation of female expository teachers."

—**Jim Shaddix**, professor of expository preaching, Southeastern Baptist Theological Seminary

"*Empowered and Equipped* is a valuable resource for any woman who finds herself teaching in the church. As women answer the call to make disciples, they must teach all that God has commanded from 'In the beginning, God' to 'Even so, come, Lord Jesus,' and everything in between. Julia Higgins has given women not only a much-needed tool for any Bible teacher who longs to rightly handle God's Word, but also an impassioned word of encouragement for women to never stop teaching women, taking them to depths of Scripture that they may know the priceless treasure God has for them.

—**Terri Stovall**, dean of women and professor of women's ministry, Southwestern Baptist Theological Seminary

"Finally, a serious resource for women who want to grow in their gifting as Bible teachers. This book is both scholarly and readable. It is a trustworthy guide for anyone who wants to learn the tasks of faithful interpretation and formational exposition."

—**Leigh Swanson**, executive vice president,
Reformed Theological Seminary, Orlando

"Operating within a solidly complementarian framework, Julia Higgins has produced a marvelous tool to furnish women with a strategic grasp of God's Word and an effective method to teach others. Engaging both the heart and the mind, relying on the Word and the Spirit, she expertly guides her readers through the world of the Bible so they can relate it in the contexts in which God has placed them. I commend the trustworthy theology and robust hermeneutic of *Empowered and Equipped* as a rich resource for the church, with confidence that everyone who reads and applies it will have greater gospel impact."

—**Hershael W. York,** dean of the school of theology,
The Southern Baptist Theological Seminary

EMPOWERED
&
EQUIPPED

EMPOWERED
&
EQUIPPED

Bible Exposition for Women
Who Teach the Scriptures

◆

JULIA B. HIGGINS
FOREWORD BY JEN WILKIN

ACADEMIC
NASHVILLE, TENNESSEE

CONTENTS

FOREWORD

by Jen Wilkin

You hold in your hands a book I wish I had held in mine twenty-three years ago. That was the year I first began to teach a small Sunday school class of women at my church. I was twenty-nine years old, younger than all of my students, and the class had fallen to me because no one else had wanted to take it on. I was terrified. And rightly so. Did I even belong there?

No matter the size of the room, when we presume to teach we should expect to be judged more strictly. Teaching is work, and 2 Tim 2:15 tells us to do our best at it, that we might be workers with no need to be ashamed. It seemed to me that if it was possible to be an unashamed worker who rightly divides the truth, it also must be possible to be an ashamed one who divides it wrongly. I very much wanted to honor the Word of God as I should, but my access to resources was minimal.

Julia Higgins has ably compiled the help I wish I had. She is a trustworthy guide, pointing the way to sound teaching as one who has shown many women that path. She brings years of experience in seminary settings to the pages of this book and offers them in accessible ways to women like I was two decades ago—compelled to start, uncertain of how to do so. A book like this would have shortened my learning curve and removed more than one shameful moment of clumsy or careless teaching. But I think it would have done more than just that.

Around the same time that I started teaching that class, my husband Jeff's roommate and best friend from college got engaged. We had remained very close with Steve after graduation, and we looked toward his wedding eagerly. We went to a couples' shower and received our wedding invitation in the mail, but I knew we were both feeling the oddness of the fact that Jeff had not been asked to be a groomsman. It felt like a glaring omission, and honestly, it stung just a bit. But we coached ourselves through the confusion and hurt, assuming the very best of our friend.

Four days before the wedding, Steve called. His fiancée was checking off tasks and had noticed that Jeff had not picked up his tuxedo. In the excitement of getting married, Steve had forgotten to ask Jeff to be a groomsman, and at some point had just assumed that he already had. The tux was hurriedly procured, and the wedding took place just as it was planned to all along, just as it should be, with Jeff standing witness beside his dear friend.

We still tease Steve about this. It's one of the funniest stories of a long friendship filled with funny stories. And yes, I did change his name to protect the not-so-innocent.

Not just anyone picks up a book like this. My guess is that you sense a call to teach and, like me, you want to be a worker unashamed. This book will equip you with excellent tools, but it also contains a message you must not miss: *you are invited.* The church needs women to teach the Bible and to do so skillfully. If someone in church leadership forgot to tell you that or assumed you would take it for granted, consider this book your explicit invitation.

Ours is no forgetful Bridegroom. Your absence among those who bear witness to the faithfulness of God is unthinkable. The favor of your presence is requested—no, required. Take your place in line and make disciples, teaching them to observe all that he has commanded. Not only do you belong here, sister, the mission does not go forward without you. Take up your tools and do the good works God ordained for you to do.

INTRODUCTION
WHY SHOULD WOMEN TEACH THE BIBLE?

One semester, a colleague asked me to visit his class on a particular day when students would be discussing discipleship. He had planned for three different student panels—one where the male students would talk about discipling men, one where female students would talk about discipling women, and one where another group would discuss cross-cultural evangelism and discipleship. My reason for being there was to spur on discussion in the class, so I didn't expect the impact one student's comments would make upon me. As the conversation turned to discipling women, typical women's events came up. A student commented that she would no longer attend discipleship events geared for women at her church because the themes were always along the lines of topics like "how to be a Proverbs 31 woman" or "modesty." With passion in her voice, she began to express a desire for women's ministry to be filled with rich biblical and theological teaching.

Her desires underscore my own because I have been in churches that have disregarded expository Bible teaching from its pastors and members alike. From birth until eighth grade, I was raised in the Episcopal Church. I have vivid memories of sitting in my Sunday school class, discussing *Saturday Night Live* from the night before while dusty Bibles sat in a closet. We would spend the hour that was supposed to be devoted to small group Bible study discussing trivial things of the world. Looking back on that experience, and comparing it with other churches that taught the Word week in and week out, it stands out to me how empty it

1

feels to attend church programs where the holy Word of God is not given prominence and the Spirit is not at work.

Thankfully, God began to work in the life of my parents, and we were led to a different church. By the beginning of my ninth grade year, my parents had both been converted to Christ and we began visiting local churches. We would eventually join a vibrant Southern Baptist church where the pastors taught through the Bible on Sunday morning, Sunday night, and Wednesday night. The church also held small groups every Sunday morning, before and after the Sunday morning service, where lay leaders taught through books of the Bible. It was in my ninth grade girls, small group where I first witnessed a woman teaching the Scriptures.

I can't remember the book of the Bible the class was studying. But I do remember my teacher, her love for Jesus and for his Word. She made the Bible come alive. She taught with passion and clarity, giving me a hunger to understand God's Word. When she taught, I recognized the authority of the Scriptures in her life as well as the soul-satisfying treasure the Bible was for her.

It was in that church, and others like it that I attended later in life, where I witnessed women teaching other women God's Word through various small group or women's ministry settings. Sometimes, the teaching was marked by expository Bible teaching, but I also began to notice that women's ministry events trended toward topical teaching that lacked biblical and theological depth. Teaching became focused on subjects related to the concept of biblical womanhood, such as how to be a good wife or mother. Messages sometimes were presented as if they were expository, but when taught, had nothing to do with the meaning of the text for the original audience and were focused mainly on broad application points that seemed unrelated and disconnected from the passage.

Biblical womanhood certainly has its place in women's ministry teaching. Teaching that conveys God's design for both genders is especially important for women in today's cultural context, and women need to be taught the importance of being made in the image of God, equal to men, and yet biologically distinct. But the emphasis that topic receives in women's ministry events often implies that being a good wife or mother is what forms women into mature disciples of Christ.

The Commission to Make Disciples: Teaching Others

The Great Commission provides a blueprint for discipleship in the church when Jesus tells the disciples, "All authority has been given to me in heaven and on earth. Go, therefore, and make disciples of all nations, baptizing them in the name of the Father and of the Son and of the Holy Spirit, teaching them to observe everything I have commanded you. And remember, I am with you always, to the end of the age" (Matt 28:18–20). Additionally, the Great Commission underscores that both men and women are commissioned to teach. A key phrase to note is "teaching them to observe everything" commanded by Jesus. The imperative command of making disciples is fulfilled when we baptize believers and incorporate them into the life of the church, teaching them the doctrines of Jesus.

What must be underscored is the popular refrain, "Make disciples, not converts." William Hendriksen contemplates this adage as he questions in his commentary on Matthew, "But just what is meant by 'make disciples'? It is not exactly the same as 'make converts,' though the latter is surely implied."[1] He concludes, "The term 'make disciples' places somewhat more stress on the fact that the mind, as well as the heart and the will, must be won for God. A disciple is *a pupil, a learner*" (emphasis his).[2] Considering that disciples are pupils or learners highlights the need for a curriculum—which Jesus identifies in the Great Commission as "everything I have commanded." The mind of the disciple must be shaped by the teachings of Christ.

The church (indicating both men and women) is commanded to go and make disciples, or learners of the doctrines taught by Jesus. If women are to be on mission, fulfilling this calling and command of the Lord Jesus, this assumes they must both be taught and be teachers. The question might remain—what is meant by Jesus when he refers to all that he has commanded? Hendriksen is helpful in identifying those elements explicitly taught by Christ:

a. All of Christ's marvelous discourses

---

[1] William Hendriksen, *New Testament Commentary: Matthew* (Grand Rapids: Baker, 2004), 999.

[2] Hendriksen, 999.

b. All of his parables; both a. and b. including ever so many "commands," whether implied or expressed. Among them are:

c. Precious "sayings," such as: "Abide in me . . . love each other . . . also bear witness" (John 15:4, 12, 27); "Love your enemies" (Matt 5:44); "Deny yourself, take up your cross, and follow me" (Luke 9:23)

d. Specific predictions and promises or assurances . . . implied directives for Christian conduct

e. The lessons of the cross, hypocrisy, proclaiming the gospel; on prayer, humility, trust, the forgiving spirit, the law

f. And is not even the narrative of Christ's sojourn on earth—the account of his healing, traveling, suffering, death, resurrection, etc.—full of implied "commands"?[3]

We must conclude then that women are commissioned by Christ alongside their brothers to make disciples, teaching all that Jesus has commanded—namely the doctrines and ethics of Christian living.

The Pattern for Teaching in the Local Church

The Great Commission reveals the broad command for all believers to teach the doctrines of Christ, and the New Testament provides guidance on how the Commission is accomplished in the local church. In Titus 1 and 2, we discern the specific commands given to pastors for doctrinal oversight of the church, as well as pastoral responsibility for gender-specific relationships which concern how doctrine is lived out. Titus 2 in particular highlights how women are assigned a teaching role within the body for the edification of other women.

The book of Titus is named after its recipient. The apostle Paul wrote his epistle to a man he designates as "my true son in our common faith" (Titus 1:4). Paul identifies himself as a servant and as an apostle, noting that his service and apostleship was "for the faith of God's elect and their knowledge of the truth that leads to godliness, in the hope of

---

[3] Hendriksen, 1002.

eternal life . . ." (Titus 1:1–2). Within verse 1, we see that Paul's ministry was missional—for the salvation of those appointed to eternal life, and for their consequent growth in a body of doctrine ("knowledge of the truth") which would influence their behavior reflected in a holy way of life ("leads to godliness").

After identifying himself and his purpose as a servant and apostle of the Lord, and after identifying Titus as the recipient of the letter, Paul immediately lists his aim, which is to remind Titus about his role: "The reason I left you in Crete was to set right what was left undone and, as I directed you, to appoint elders in every town" (Titus 1:5). Paul commissioned Titus to appoint elders (or pastors) for the churches in Crete. He recaps for Titus the specific credentials of an elder in verses 6–9 (which includes that an elder be "the husband of one wife," indicating that the position of pastor/elder is reserved for qualified men). He then contrasts the characteristics of elders with those of false teachers who were found at that time in Crete (vv. 10–14).

Part of Paul's own commission as an apostle (for the knowledge of the truth among the elect) is to be reiterated in the lives of appointed, qualified local church pastors. Elders are to be found "holding to the faithful message as taught, so that [they] will be able both to encourage sound teaching and to refute those who contradict it" (v. 9). Pastors must hold to a body of doctrine for two-fold effect upon the church: encouragement to hold to sound teaching and the repudiation of false doctrine. Thus, Paul tells Titus in 2:1, "But you are to proclaim things consistent with sound teaching" (CSB) or rather he is to "teach what accords with sound doctrine" (ESV).

It is within the context of Paul's emphasizing elders who will teach and protect sound doctrine that the foundation is laid for gender-specific teaching/discipleship within the body. In the second chapter of Titus, verses 2 and following, Paul instructs Titus to make sure that the entire church is involved in the task of teaching that influences godly behavior. He designates gender-specific discipleship to accomplish that task, as he discusses older and younger men and older and younger women. Notice that older men are to "be sound in faith" (v. 2) and older women are to "teach what is good" (v. 3).

Thus, we conclude that pastors/elders have been given a task of overseeing the teaching ministry of the church. They are the chief teachers, disseminating and protecting the doctrine that is taught in a local body, making sure to expose false teaching, and encouraging members to hold to sound teaching that then leads to a godly life. Pastors/elders are given the task of making sure that men and women alike are sound and teaching what is good.

When pairing the concepts of the Great Commission and the Titus 2 passage, we cannot miss that women have been given a teaching role within the church, and that role is meant to be exercised in the context of discipleship. The Bible also teaches us that while all are commanded to disciple, some are especially empowered by the Holy Spirit with a gift of teaching.

Empowered to Teach

The New Testament contains various texts on the topic of spiritual gifts within the church. Romans 12 and 1 Corinthians 12 are the two most significant passages written concerning gifts of grace that are given to believers by the Holy Spirit. The table below illustrates the various gifts:

1 Corinthians 12:7–11	1 Corinthians 12:28	Romans 12:6–8
Wisdom	Apostles	Prophecy
Knowledge	Prophets	Service
Faith	Teachers	Teaching
Healing	Miracles	Exhorting
Miracles	Healings	Giving
Prophecy	Helping	Leading
Discernment	Leading	Mercy
Tongues	Tongues	
Interpretation of Tongues	Interpretation of Tongues	

Commentators consistently remark that the list of gifts given is not exhaustive, but Paul was identifying ways individual members of the church might be empowered for the purpose of serving and building up other members of the church. Paul's emphasis in both Romans 12 and 1 Corinthians 12 is that the body has been equipped with a diversity of giftings to manifest God's Spirit for the common good (1 Cor 12:7). Each person in the church has been empowered to serve others according to how the Spirit willed a gift to them (1 Cor 12:11). That means that the Godhead, through the Spirit, has a particular gift in mind for every particular person so that the work of the Holy Spirit and God's grace are manifested within the local church.

Some may conflate the spiritual gift of teaching with the office of pastor/elder and draw a false conclusion that only men are to exercise the gift of teaching. While qualified men are responsible to teach and oversee the local church, that does not negate the fact that both men and women are given the spiritual gift of teaching. Thus, John Frame distinguishes between two types of teaching that are seen in the New Testament— special-office teaching and general-office teaching:

> The overseers are given particular responsibility for teaching, but there is also a sense in which every Christian is a teacher (Eph 4:29; Col 3:16; Heb 5:12; 1 John 2:27). In Reformed theology, the official teaching is said to belong to the *special office*, while the teaching of all believers is part of the *general office*, that is, the priesthood of all believers. Special-office teaching requires special gifts of character and competence (1 Tim 3:1–7), and (as I understand 1 Timothy 2:12) that teaching is restricted to men only. Women may and do participate in general-office teaching, however, as when Priscilla (mentioned first, most likely, to indicate her prominence in this activity) partners with her husband Aquila to instruct Apollos in the word of God (Acts 18:26), and as when Paul instructs older women to teach younger women (Titus 2:2–5).[4]

---

[4] John M. Frame, *The Doctrine of the Word of God*, vol. 4 of *A Theology of Lordship* (Phillipsburg, NJ: P&R Publishing, 2010), 259.

Three women of the New Testament illustrate the concept of women teaching for the upbuilding of other believers: Mary, Lois, and Eunice. These women display general-office teaching that many women are called to today.

New Testament Examples of Women Teaching

In Luke 1:46–55, Mary sings a hymn of praise to God in front of her cousin, Elizabeth. This hymn was recorded by Luke and since that time, it has been used in worship services throughout the ages. Consider how the apostle Paul instructs the church at Colossae to *teach one another* through the use of hymns: "Let the word of Christ dwell richly among you, in all wisdom teaching and admonishing one another through psalms, hymns, and spiritual songs, singing to God with gratitude in your hearts" (Col 3:16). Mary's hymn is an excellent example of a woman worshiping God through a hymn, which had the immediate benefit of edifying another believer (Elizabeth) as she stood by, as well as teaching the church through its liturgical incorporation as the "Magnificat" throughout church history.

The contents of Mary's hymn reveal that she was well versed in Old Testament Scripture. While there are references to Genesis, Deuteronomy, Psalms, Isaiah, Zephaniah, and Malachi, Mary's words parallel the prayer of Hannah found in 1 Sam 2:1–10. Hannah's prayer begins, "My heart rejoices in the LORD; my horn is lifted up by the LORD," while Mary's begins, "My soul magnifies the Lord, and my spirit rejoices in God my Savior" (Luke 1:46–47). Surely Mary, being a young woman who was told she was with child and who knew her Old Testament, was thinking back to Hannah, who also praised the Lord for how he had answered her prayer for a son. While Mary does not mention Gen 3:15, it is likely she would have been thinking of the promise given to Eve that the offspring of the woman would crush the head of the serpent. The women of Israel had been looking for this promised offspring since the days of the garden, and because this hope was being realized, Mary proclaims, "Surely, from now on all generations will call me blessed" (v. 48). Mary's hymn teaches us the character of God as she reflects upon her personal situation and the future for the people of God (vv. 50–55). Her words model that of a psalm, as Robert Stein notes in *The New American Commentary* on Luke, "For a hymn or psalm to begin with an individual's situation and conclude with a reference to Israel's situation is not unusual."[5] This entire section of Luke gives evidence of a woman who knew the Scriptures and was interpreting and applying them appropriately to her situation, with the added benefit of teaching her cousin, Elizabeth, and all believers who would go on to sing the Magnificat.

Another example of learned women comes from that of Lois and Eunice, the mother and grandmother of Paul's protégé, Timothy. The book of 2 Timothy, written by Paul to Timothy at the end of his ministry, gives us insight into these two women and provides a pattern for women teaching sound doctrine to their children. Hendriksen notes that the theme of 2 Timothy is that of sound doctrine, and he provides a brief, memorable outline of the entire book: "HOLD ON TO IT Chapter 1, TEACH IT Chapter 2, ABIDE IN IT Chapter 3, PREACH IT Chapter 4."[6] In 2 Tim 1:5, Paul mentions Timothy's relatives by recalling Timothy's "sincere faith that first lived in your grandmother Lois and in your mother Eunice and now, I am convinced, is in you also." Later, in chapter 3, Paul instructs Timothy to abide in sound doctrine, reminding him of those who have taught him the Scriptures from childhood (vv. 14–15). Hendriksen conveys that Paul, Lois, and Eunice were used by God to instruct Timothy in the faith:

> Timothy must never forget that he had learned these things from no less a person than Paul himself (see verses 10 and 11 above) and, going back even farther, from those highly esteemed worthies: grandmother Lois and mother Eunice (II Tim. 1:5), women who, before their conversion to the Christian faith, had instructed the little child Timothy in "the sacred writings," and who, having once accepted Jesus as their Lord and Savior, had

---

[5] Robert H. Stein, *The New American Commentary: Luke* (Nashville: B&H, 1992), 93.

[6] William Hendriksen, *New Testament Commentary: Exposition of the Pastoral Epistles, II Timothy* (Grand Rapids: Baker, 2004), 219.

been used as instruments in God's hand to co-operate with Paul in the important task of leading the young man to see in Christ the fulfilment of the Old Testament promises.

It is clear that Paul, Lois, and Eunice, and any others who may have nurtured Timothy, are not viewed as independent authorities, apart from the Word, but as secondary or intermediate sources of knowledge, avenues of instruction, and even this *only because they accepted the Scripture!*[7]

Paul, the apostle, handing off his ministry to Timothy, reminds the young pastor to never forget what he has been taught by not only the apostle himself, but also his mother and grandmother. This charge from Paul highlights an important implication: women must be equipped to teach sound doctrine to those in their sphere of influence.

Equipped to Teach

A common adage states that women typically make up more than half the church. This observation is not true of only the US church but reflects the global church, as Lifeway Research notes, "Globally, the weekly church attendance gender gap remains an issue. Among the 53 nations Pew analyzed with enough Christian respondents, there is an average difference of 7 percentage points between men (46 percent) and women (53 percent)."[8] While Lifeway Research notes that in the United States "for decades, women have been more likely to attend church than men" they comment that in "recent years the gap has been shrinking—but it's not necessarily good news."[9] The reason a decrease in the gender gap is considered bad news is because the number of women attending church weekly is in decline. Lifeway cites a General Social Survey conducted by

---

[7] Hendriksen, 295–96.

[8] Aaron Earls, "Church Attendance Gender Gap Shrinks, but It's Not All Good News," Lifeway Research, September 25, 2017, https://lifewayresearch .com/2017/09/25/church-attendance-gender-gap-shrinks-but-its-not-all-good -news/.

[9] Earls.

Pew Research from 1972–2014 which reveals that female church attendance has steadily regressed from 38 percent in the early 1980s to 28 percent in 2012.

The downward trend of weekly church attendance of both genders should awaken Christian men and women to a recommitment to the work of the Great Commission. Jesus told us to go and make disciples, literal learners, and teach them all that Jesus commands. His commission is a charge that women of the church must take seriously. The New Testament gives us the main pattern for how we should disciple, and that comes from Titus 2. Older godly women are to be teaching what is good in the context of gender-distinct discipling environments. But not only that, we cannot ignore that gifts of grace have been given to women to serve and edify the body, and this includes the spiritual gift of teaching. Women like Mary, Lois, and Eunice reveal to us that women should know the Scriptures and should handle them well, because their influence extends to the entire church. Because of these reasons, women in the church must be equipped to teach.

When a woman attends seminary to get a master's degree, no matter the degree program, she will be required to take a course that prepares her to teach the Bible. But not all women have the opportunity to go to seminary. This book seeks to prepare women in the local church who are committed to the Great Commission, who are making disciples, or who have been given the spiritual gift of teaching.

The book is divided into two parts: principles and practice. In the first part, we will consider the importance of core characteristics of the Bible and will introduce the concept of biblical theology, along with how to interpret passages of Scripture based upon genre. We will also explore what is known as the historical-grammatical method of interpretation, seeking to understand the best means for determining a text's meaning so that it may then be taught properly.

In the second part of the book, we will discover what it looks like to apply what we have learned by considering practical elements of teaching. Spiritual disciplines, a lifestyle that should mark every Christian, will be considered as the foundation for solid biblical teaching. We will also discuss core doctrines of the faith, our commitment to those doctrines, and teaching within the bounds of orthodoxy. Finally, the last chapter will explore the various avenues for women to teach in the local church. It is my hope and prayer that as you delve into these matters, more so than ever, you will be equipped to teach.

1

The Nature of the Bible

Your word is a lamp for my feet and a light on my path.
—Psalm 119:105

From my childhood, the Lord has providentially placed his written Word in my life, and looking back, I can see that the Father was pursuing me through the Bible to reveal his Son, Jesus, to me. When I was around the age of five, someone gave me a record album that had the creation account and other biblical stories on it. I recall sitting on my bedroom floor, listening to that album all alone and becoming fascinated with stories from Scripture that I had never heard. As I grew a little older, my grandmother took me to the United Methodist Church she attended and bought a New American Standard Bible for me from the bookstore. I would read that Bible from time to time, but it was difficult to read, and I did not understand much of what it said. Around that same period, the Gideons distributed small Bibles at my school when I was in second or third grade. I would read the plan of salvation in the back cover of that small, green Bible and I would pray the sinner's prayer over and over. And while I was not truly converted at that point, God was using his Word, incrementally, to disclose himself to me.

The Bible is the most fascinating book that has ever been penned because it unveils a transcendent, powerful, holy, and righteous God. It reveals an infinite God to a finite people. According to his grace and by his divine initiative, he has chosen to reveal himself by imparting the written Word through the Holy Spirit, and he has preserved and used his words to show himself to his people for thousands of years. He employs the Scriptures to call us to salvation, to sanctify us, and to bring joy to our hearts as we traverse various trials of life. This chapter will discuss the means of revelation used by our triune God to communicate himself to his people and will demonstrate the nature of the Bible (its core characteristics).

The Revelation of God

Various Scriptures communicate the ways God has revealed himself, but one of the preeminent texts that systematic theologians appeal to when they teach the doctrine of revelation is Psalm 19. This psalm of David can be divided into two segments that reflect the concepts known as 1) general revelation and 2) special revelation.

General revelation is the act of God whereby he reveals himself through the created order. The triune God is made known as humans reflect on the world around them. Psalm 19:1–4 teaches that

> The heavens declare the glory of God,
> and the expanse proclaims the work of his hands.
> Day after day they pour out speech;
> night after night they communicate knowledge.
> There is no speech; there are no words;
> their voice is not heard.
> Their message has gone out to the whole earth,
> and their words to the ends of the world.

In Psalm 19, David praises the Lord for the work of creation because the heavens (the sky, the expanse) proclaim to all of humankind that there is a God, and this God is glorious. The work of God's hands testifies daily that there is a God who exists and who has fashioned this beautiful world with its bright colors and wonderful mountains, lakes, deserts, valleys, flowers, trees, and animals to exhibit his glory, power, and creativity. Paul, writing to the church at Rome in Rom 1:20, considers general revelation when he teaches that man has no excuse for unbelief because creation sets the character of God on display for all to see: "For his invisible attributes, that is, his eternal power and divine nature, have been clearly seen since the creation of the world, being understood through what he has made. As a result, people are without excuse." General revelation—the act whereby God reveals himself through nature—is a key way God communicates his existence to every single person on the planet. Although God's glory is revealed through creation, it is limited in what it communicates for one cannot glimpse nature and come to know the love of God in Christ and the salvation he extends to all humankind.

God has chosen to reveal himself not only generally through creation but also particularly, through his Word. After David speaks about the revealing of the Lord through creation in Psalm 19, he goes on to consider the specific ways God makes himself known through the Scriptures in verses 7–11:

> The instruction of the Lord is perfect,
> renewing one's life;
> the testimony of the Lord is trustworthy,
> making the inexperienced wise.
> The precepts of the Lord are right,
> making the heart glad;
> the command of the Lord is radiant,
> making the eyes light up.
> The fear of the Lord is pure,
> enduring forever;
> the ordinances of the Lord are reliable
> and altogether righteous.
> They are more desirable than gold—
> than an abundance of pure gold;
> and sweeter than honey

dripping from a honeycomb.

In addition, your servant is warned by them,

and in keeping them there is an abundant reward.

Notice the five terms that David assigns to God's Word: instruction, testimonies, precepts, commands, and ordinances. All of these terms encapsulate the various forms of Scripture available to David during his lifetime. When David was writing, he did not have the completed Bible that is accessible today, for the completed Bible or *canon* (that is, the sixty-six compiled books that make up the Bible) had not been assembled in its more modern form. As David wrote Psalm 19 and meditated upon the characteristics of the Word of God, he was likely contemplating the books of the law, known as the *Torah*. The word for law or instruction in verse 7 is the Hebrew word, *torah*. In Calvin's commentary on the book of Psalms, the significance of David's use of the word *torah* (or "law") is explored:

> Under the term law, he not only means the rule of living righteously, or the Ten Commandments, but he also comprehends the covenant by which God had distinguished that people from the rest of the world, and the whole doctrine of Moses, the parts of which he afterwards enumerates under the terms testimonies, statutes, and other names. These titles and commendations by which he exalts the dignity and excellence of the Law would not agree with the Ten Commandments alone, unless there were, at the same time, joined to them a free adoption and the promises which depend upon it; and, in short, the whole body of doctrine of which true religion and godliness consists.[1]

The covenant, or the "whole doctrine of Moses" Calvin suggests that David understood, includes the books of Genesis, Exodus, Leviticus, Numbers, and Deuteronomy. These five books were what David assigns as instruction, testimonies, precepts, commands, and ordinances that he then pronounces perfect, trustworthy, right, radiant, pure, reliable, and

---

[1] John Calvin and James Anderson, *Commentary on the Book of Psalms*, vol 1. (Bellingham, WA: Faithlife), 318.

altogether righteous. These seven descriptors of God's Word communicate something of its nature:

> *It is Perfect*—meaning "complete, sound"[2]
>
> *It is Trustworthy*—meaning "sure, fixed, firm, stable"[3]
>
> *It is Right*—meaning "morally right, straight"[4]
>
> *It is Radiant*—meaning "spotless, clean, without fault"[5]
>
> *It is Pure*—meaning "ethically pure, clean"[6]
>
> *It is Reliable*—meaning "firm, faithful"[7]
>
> *It is Altogether Righteous*—meaning that "the entire Law, which is from first to last [is] 'exceedingly righteous and true.'"[8]

As David employs these seven adjectives to describe the Torah, so too theologians adopt descriptors that highlight the perfection, trustworthiness, rightness, radiance, purity, reliability, and altogether righteousness of the entire Bible. These descriptors or characteristics are explored in the following section which highlights the nature of the Bible.

Core Characteristics of Scripture

For women who aspire to serve the local church through the general-teaching office (mentioned in the introduction, "Why Should Women Teach the Bible?"), the first step toward being equipped to teach is a

---

[2] Robert L. Thomas, *New American Standard Hebrew-Aramaic and Greek Dictionaries*, updated ed. (La Habra, CA: Foundation, 1998).

[3] H. D. M. Spence, *Psalms*, vol. 1 (New York: Funk & Wagnalls, 1909), 129.

[4] Derek Kidner, *Psalms 1–72: An Introduction and Commentary*, vol. 1 (Downers Grove, IL: IVP Academic, 1973), 117.

[5] Spence, *Psalms*, vol. 1, 130.

[6] Francis Brown, Samuel Driver, and Charles Augustus, *Enhanced Brown-Driver-Briggs Hebrew and English Lexicon* (Oxford, UK: Clarendon, 1977), 141.

[7] Thomas, *New American Standard Hebrew-Aramaic and Greek Dictionaries*.

[8] Spence, *Psalms*, vol. 1, 130.

study of the nature of God's Word. A blunt question is relevant to consider: What is your doctrine of the Word? Women, alongside their brothers in Christ, should study and articulate what they believe about special revelation because "the Bible, or more accurately our attitude toward the Bible, is a watershed issue in Christian teaching. The Bible teacher's view of Scripture will serve to determine the direction and purpose of his [or her] teaching ministry."[9] A teacher of God's Word will not rightly divide the Scriptures if she has a faulty understanding of the nature of the Bible itself. For example, if a teacher of the Bible has not contemplated, explored, and developed a belief in the truthfulness and reliability of the Scriptures, the teacher may not place as great a weight as needed upon obedience to the commands given to Christians for lack of belief in the Bible's inerrant and sufficient nature.

Therefore, readers must consider their ability to define and defend the Bible as inspired, inerrant, infallible, clear, necessary, sufficient, and authoritative. This section will explore each of those core characteristics of Scripture.

Inspired

The inspiration of Scripture is defined as "the work in which God by His Spirit, through human writers, gave us His Word. The origin of Scripture is divine."[10] The Bible itself attests to the fact that it is divinely inspired, or rather that the ultimate origin of the Bible is from God himself. This truth is explicitly taught by the apostle Paul when he reminds Timothy that "all Scripture is inspired by God" (2 Tim 3:16). This small verse contains significant information regarding the divine origin of the Bible. First, Paul uses the word "all" to reveal that every single word and everything in the original manuscripts is inspired. The

---

[9] Lawrence O. Richards and Gary J. Bredfeldt, *Creative Bible Teaching* (Chicago: Moody, 2020), 21.

[10] The Chicago Statement on Biblical Inerrancy, Article VII, https://www.thegospelcoalition.org/themelios/article/the-chicago-statement-on-biblical-inerrancy/.

technical wording theologians use for this belief is *verbal plenary inspiration*. Verbal "means that the *words* of Scripture, not only the ideas of the biblical writers, are God's Word."[11] Plenary means "that *everything* in Scripture is God's Word."[12]

The second word Paul uses in 2 Tim 3:16 is "Scripture," which in Greek is *graphe*, meaning "the writings." The verse ends with a phrase: "inspired by God." The literal rendering of this phrase in Greek is "breathed out." The text is teaching that all the writings of Scripture are inspired because they have been breathed out or spoken by God.

While 2 Tim 3:16 enables us to understand the divine origin of the Bible, the apostle Peter comes alongside Paul to underscore God's incorporation of human authors to compose the words he intended. Peter reminds his recipients: "Above all, you know this: No prophecy of Scripture comes from the prophet's own interpretation, because no prophecy ever came by the will of man; instead, men spoke from God as they were carried along by the Holy Spirit" (2 Pet 1:20–21). Peter teaches that God inspired human authors through the work of the Holy Spirit. In his commentary on 2 Peter, Thomas Schreiner reflects on this concept:

> Human beings spoke, and they spoke with their own personalities and literary styles; hence inspiration does not require a dictation theory of inspiration. The words the prophets spoke, however, ultimately came from God. They were inspired, or "carried along," by the Holy Spirit. Hence, Peter defended the accuracy of the prophecies in the Scriptures. Note that v. 20 speaks of "prophecy of Scripture," so Peter's words cannot be limited to oral prophecies.[13]

---

[11] Frame, *The Doctrine of the Word of God*, 143 (see introduction, n. 4).

[12] Frame, 143.

[13] Thomas Schreiner, *New American Commentary 1, 2 Peter, Jude*, vol. 37 (Nashville: B&H, 2003), 324.

The Chicago Statement on Biblical Inerrancy, Article VIII upholds both God's authorship of the Bible as well as human authorship by offering both an affirmation and a pertinent denial:

> *We affirm that God in His Work of inspiration utilized the distinctive personalities and literary styles of the writers whom He had chosen and prepared.*

> *We deny that God, in causing these writers to use the very words that He chose, overrode their personalities.*

What both Schreiner and the Chicago Statement on Biblical Inerrancy affirm about the inspiration of Scripture is critical to understand: God communicates to men and women through a distinct process which includes his own personal words revealed to humankind through human authors. John Frame, building upon work done by Kuyper and Bavinck, highlights that the process could be termed "organic inspiration" which means "God used the differences of heredity, environment, upbringing, education, gifts, talents, styles, interests, and idiosyncrasies to reveal his word. . . . God used the organic complexity of human persons and the diversities among persons to communicate . . . with us in a fully personal way."[14] The method God employs for special revelation is distinct and personal; consequently, the Bible teacher who understands the concept of divine inspiration may find joy in the God who has spoken and who has a divine word to impart to the humans he has created.

Inerrant

If the Bible is divine inspiration given to us by the triune God, it follows then that the divinely inspired words are incapable of deceiving us. God, who is true and is the standard of all truth, only speaks words which are true, for "it is impossible for God to lie . . ." (Heb 6:18). Accordingly, the concept of inerrancy finds its foundation in inspiration.[15] Inerrancy

---

[14] Frame, *The Doctrine of the Word of God*, 142.

[15] The Chicago Statement on Biblical Inerrancy, Article XV.

is defined by the Chicago Statement on Biblical Inerrancy to mean that Scripture is "free from all falsehood, fraud, or deceit."[16] Proverbs 30:5 teaches that "every word of God is pure" while Ps 18:30 pairs the perfection of God with the purity, then, of his Word, "God—his way is perfect; the word of the LORD is pure." In Prov 30:5 and Ps 18:30, the word for "pure" in the original language implies testing or refinement, hinting that the words of the Torah are as pure as if they have been "refined by fire."[17]

Bible teachers should comprehend that the term *inerrancy* 1) applies specifically to the original manuscripts of the Bible and 2) pertains to current translations. Every Bible translation that exists today has been translated from various Greek, Hebrew, and Aramaic texts that are copies of the original manuscripts penned by writers of Old and New Testament books. While none of the original manuscripts are available at present, "it may first be stated that for over 99 percent of the words of the Bible, we know what the original manuscript said."[18] Thus, Wayne Grudem succinctly concludes regarding the inerrancy of the Bible translations available in modern times: "Our present manuscripts are for most purposes the same as the original manuscripts, and the doctrine of inerrancy therefore directly concerns our present manuscripts as well."[19] Therefore, when Christian scholars and pastors discuss the term *inerrancy*, the usual application is both to the original manuscripts of biblical texts but also with strong conviction about and trust in the veracity of translated copies available throughout the world today.

Since God's Word is pure and is free from deceiving, the truth of inerrancy implies first and foremost that God's Word is the preeminent source of truth that supersedes all others. Teachers of the Scriptures may rely heavily upon commentaries and study Bibles, but it is the Bible alone that offers pure insight into the person of God and his plan for this

---

[16] The Chicago Statement on Biblical Inerrancy, Article XII.

[17] H. D. M. Spence, *Proverbs* (New York: Funk and Wagnalls Co., 1909), 572.

[18] Wayne Grudem, *Systematic Theology: An Introduction to Biblical Doctrine* (Grand Rapids: Zondervan, 2020), 92.

[19] Grudem, 92–93.

world.[20] In the realm of women's Bible studies and the ministry of teaching employed by female Bible teachers, an understanding of and commitment to inerrancy underscores the necessity of women being equipped to teach. If the Bible alone is free from falsehood or deceit, then every Bible teacher should explore the tools for interpreting the Scriptures so that they may (1) teach rightly, and (2) discern when other teachers and/ or curricula do not engage in the faithful exposition and interpretation of God's Word.

Infallible

If the Bible is both inspired by God and inerrant in its nature, it follows then that the Bible is infallible, defined as "being free from or incapable of error."[21] In other words, "The infallibility of Scripture teaches that all of Scripture far from misleading us . . . is true and reliable in all the matters it addresses."[22] The term *infallible* may sound similar to *inerrant*, which is a wise observation. To understand the distinction between inerrancy and infallibility, one must consider the slight nuances of each definition: inerrancy teaches that the Bible is in the "condition of being free from error" while infallibility teaches the same concept but also adds that the Bible is *incapable of erring*.[23] Thus, these two definitions pair together because "it is impossible for the Bible to be at the same time infallible and errant in its assertions. Infallibility and inerrancy may be distinguished, but not separated."[24] A commitment to the Scriptures as divinely inspired calls one to a belief in the synonymous truths that the Bible is both inerrant and infallible.

---

[20] Daniel L. Akin, Bill Curtis, and Stephen Rummage, *Engaging Exposition* (Nashville: B&H Academic, 2011), 237.

[21] James D. Hernando, *Dictionary of Hermeneutics* (Springfield, MO: Gospel Publishing, 2012), 164.

[22] The Chicago Statement on Biblical Inerrancy, Article XI.

[23] Hernando, *Dictionary of Hermeneutics*, 163–64.

[24] The Chicago Statement on Biblical Inerrancy, Article XI.

The twin concepts of inerrancy and infallibility are affirmed based upon the Bible's presentation of itself as truth. In the Psalms, the truthfulness of God's Word is a repeated meditation for God's people. Consider Psalm 119 which proclaims,

Your law is true. (v. 142)

All your commandments are true. (v. 151)

The entirety of your word is truth. (v. 160)

Not only does the Bible assert its truthfulness, but Jesus upholds the idea, as well. In John 17, Jesus prays for the disciples and for those who would believe after them that God would "sanctify them by the truth." Jesus follows his request with the simple declaration, "Your word is truth" (v. 17). Because God has spoken, using written revelation as his means, that revelation is reliable and trustworthy; and God has a plan for the truths he has revealed, mainly that his Word be employed to bring about godliness in the life of believers. D. A. Carson, commenting on this verse in John's Gospel, highlights the truthfulness of revelation and the influence of truth upon the sanctification process of Christians: "The means Jesus expects his Father to use as he sanctifies his Son's followers is the *truth*. The Father will immerse Jesus's followers in the revelation of himself in his Son; he will sanctify them by sending the Paraclete to guide them into all *truth* (15:13). Jesus's followers will be 'set apart' from the world, reserved for God's service, insofar as they think and live in conformity with the *truth*, the 'word' of revelation (v. 6)"[25] (emphasis added).

In a world full of deceit, ever since the serpent approached Eve, beckoning and tempting her to doubt the truthfulness of God's Word, Bible teachers are called to stand upon the inerrancy and infallibility of the Scriptures. Why? Because God's special revelation is the means by which God sanctifies believers and is the only source of knowing God, what he requires of mankind, how he has intervened to save a people for himself, and what he plans to do in the future. If one has no conviction or trust

---

[25] D. A. Carson, *The Gospel According to John*, Pillar New Testament Commentary Series (Grand Rapids: Eerdmans, 1991), 566.

in the truthfulness of the Scriptures, then the entire Christian system of belief is called into question. Yet, if the Bible is God's Word, if it does not contain error, and if it is incapable of error, the next assumption is that the Scriptures are authoritative for all of life.

Authoritative

The continued study of the core characteristics of the Bible reminds us that God's Word is what it is to the believer because of the nature of the God who inspired it. To understand the authoritative nature of the Bible, one must first recognize the omnipotent character of God. The word *omnipotence* describes the power that God exerts over all creation and underscores the scriptural descriptions of God as the Almighty. In Rev 1:8, the apostle John conveys the vision of God that he is given with a sentence from God himself describing his very nature: "'I am the Alpha and the Omega,' says the Lord God, 'the one who is, who was, and who is to come, the Almighty.'" In that one verse alone, God's preeminence, eternality, and power are revealed. The word, *almighty*, literally means "all-powerful, omnipotent one."[26] His power is on display in the book of Revelation, as he is revealed as the transcendent God who wields control over all history from start to finish. The authoritative, powerful nature of God results in one reaction from redeemed humanity: worship around his throne that exalts him as the one to whom blessing, honor, glory, and power are due (Rev 5:13).

This God who is revealed as almighty, all-powerful, and omnipotent demands not only worship but also obedience of living. As he reveals himself through divine inspiration, Christians come to personally know the Almighty and the desires he has for those who follow him. The Holy Spirit works in the life of the believer to bring about obedience to God's commands. Yet, those who walk in disobedience to God's Word

---

[26] Frederick W. Danker, ed. *A Greek-English Lexicon of the New Testament and Other Early Christian Literature*, 3rd ed. (BDAG) (Chicago: University of Chicago, 2001), 755.

are essentially disobeying God.[27] This detail helps to define scriptural authority as an acknowledgment that the Bible is the supreme, final standard of truth to which the Christian submits. The book of James reminds believers to "be doers of the word and not hearers only" (Jas 1:22). The "doer" of God's Word is promised blessing "in what he does" (Jas 1:25). First John connects obedience to God's Word with being a true follower of Jesus: "This is how we know him: if we keep his commands. The one who says, 'I have come to know him,' and yet doesn't keep his commands, is a liar, and the truth is not in him. But whoever keeps his word, truly in him the love of God is made complete. This is how we know we are in him" (1 John 2:3–5). Thus, a Bible teacher understands the authoritative role the Bible has for Jesus followers and seeks to understand all that Scripture has to say, so both she and those whom she teaches may walk in obedience to all it requires.

Necessary

Defining the term *necessary* in relation to the Scriptures "is simply to say that we need it."[28]

In the Gospel of John, the necessity of Scripture is put on greatest display as Jesus interacts with his disciples. John 6 reveals that some who followed Jesus decided to turn away and no longer follow him. The text says that after the others left, "Jesus said to the Twelve, 'You don't want to go away too, do you?' Simon Peter answered, 'Lord, to whom will we go? You have the words of eternal life. We have come to believe and know that you are the Holy One of God'" (John 6:67–69). Peter's reason that the Twelve dare not turn away is twofold: Jesus has the words of eternal life, and he is the Holy One of God.

When one ponders the nature of special revelation and considers that God has used the written Word to communicate himself to people, the ultimate deduction is that the very words of God are necessary, primarily for eternal life. Peter realized this truth and connected the Word

---

[27] Grudem, *Systematic Theology*, 71.
[28] Frame, *The Doctrine of the Word of God*, 211.

of God with the Word incarnate, Christ. John Frame explores the connection between the written Word and Christ, and its salvific import for the believer:

> People often claim to have a personal relationship to Christ, while being uncertain about the role of Scripture in that relationship. But the relationship that Christ has established with his people is a covenant relationship and therefore a verbal relationship, among other things. Jesus' words, today, are found only in Scripture. So, if we are to have a covenant relationship with Jesus, we must acknowledge Scripture as his Word. No Scripture, no Lord. No Scripture, no Christ. And no Scripture, no salvation.[29]

Frame's logic cannot be dismissed for the teacher of the Bible. The necessity of Scripture for the salvation and discipleship of souls inevitability implies commitment to the Bible as the core curriculum to be mined, cherished, loved, and disseminated for the upbuilding of fellow believers.

Sufficient

Meditation upon the details of the Bible's nature brings joy to the heart. After exploring the many attributes of Scripture, with the most precious being the necessity of God's Word for eternal life, one finds delight in the fact that if the Bible is indeed necessary, then God has met that need with a Word that is entirely sufficient. Sufficiency is "the affirmation that Scripture is itself sufficient for doctrine and life (2 Tim 3:16–17) inasmuch as the Scriptures are learned with the illuminating assistance of the Holy Spirit (John 14:26; 16:13; 1 Cor 1:6ff.) and life is lived by the empowerment of the Holy Spirit (2 Pet 1:3)."[30] Second Timothy 3:16–17 are the verses most often used to demonstrate the sufficiency of the Scriptures, and it is helpful to consider exactly what those verses state about the satisfactory nature of God's Word. Paul wrote this epistle

---

[29] Frame, 212.

[30] David S. Dockery and David P. Nelson, "Special Revelation," in *A Theology for the Church* (Nashville: B&H Academic, 2007), 163.

at the end of his ministry and used his letter to encourage and build up a young pastor named Timothy. As Paul labors to "pass the baton" to an upcoming leader, he tells the young pastor to remember that God's Word is "profitable for teaching, for rebuking, for correcting, for training in righteousness, so that the man of God may be complete, equipped for every good work." When Paul describes the Bible as "profitable," what he is saying is that its "value is unparalleled and indeed essential to the Christian pastoral task."[31]

While this text specifically applies to pastoral ministry—the Bible is sufficient for the tasks of pastoring and preaching—one may deduce an application point that the Bible is the direct source for every believer to go to and find teaching (doctrine), rebuke ("reproof that is either personal or doctrinal"), correction ("revealing error and restoring to the right path"), and training ("moral training that leads to righteous living").[32] This principle is underscored by 2 Pet 1:3–4, which explains that God's "divine power has given us everything required for life and godliness through the knowledge of him who called us by his own glory and goodness. By these he has given us very great and precious promises . . ." Peter connects the idea of God's "divine power" which is sufficient for life and godliness with "his very great and precious promises." Christ is able to provide all that believers need for eternal life and for a godly life on earth, through our knowledge of him, through his promises. Surely, the Word of God outlines and details every great and precious promise of Christ, and it is sufficient for the task of calling believers to salvation and godly living.

Clear

The clarity of the Scriptures, also referred to as "perspicuity" by theologians, may be defined as "the belief that the words of Scripture are sufficiently clear (perspicuous) so that the competent Christian can read and

---

[31] Robert W. Yarbrough, *The Letters to Timothy and Titus* (PNTC) (Grand Rapids: Eerdmans, 2018), 430.

[32] Hayne P. Griffin Jr. and Thomas D. Lea, *1, 2 Timothy, Titus: An Exegetical and Theological Exposition of Scripture* (NAC) (Nashville: B&H, 1992), 237.

understand its redemptive message without the need for church tradition as an official guide."[33] You may immediately be reminded of times of confusion or misunderstanding while reading the Scriptures, for the Bible does contain material that is difficult to grasp. For example, concepts and dialogue found within the book of Job can be unclear to those who do not seek assistance from commentaries or study Bibles. The perspicuous nature of God's Word does allow for difficulty in understanding.

When thinking about perspicuity, one must understand that the doctrine applies to clarity surrounding knowledge of salvation and the need for guidance from the Holy Spirit. Charles Hodge explains,

> It is not denied that the Scriptures contain many things hard to be understood; that they require diligent study; that all men need the guidance of the Holy Spirit in order to right knowledge and true faith. But it is maintained that in all things necessary to salvation they are sufficiently plain to be understood even by the unlearned.[34]

Thus, the Scriptures are not only necessary to know about salvation, are not only sufficient to teach about salvation, but they are written in such a way that they are clear concerning salvation. Still, the work of the Spirit must be underscored. Bible teachers who believe in the necessity, sufficiency, and clarity of God's Word are totally dependent upon God's Spirit to help them understand the truths the Scriptures convey.

Conclusion

This chapter discussed the revelation of God, both general and special. The nature of the Bible, that it is inspired, inerrant, infallible, authoritative, necessary, sufficient, and clear, has been defined, allowing you to contemplate the Bible's core characteristics in relation to teaching the Bible and in the context of ministry to women. While this chapter considered

---

[33] Hernando, *Dictionary of Hermeneutics*, 31.

[34] Charles Hodge, *Systematic Theology*, vol. I (New York: Scribner, Armstrong and Co., 1873), 183.

the main identifying features of the Bible, two important characteristics have not been explored: its unity and its Christotelic storyline. Chapter 2 advances an understanding of God's Word by revealing the importance of biblical theology for teaching the Word.

2

The Overarching Story of the Bible

Then beginning with Moses and all the Prophets, he interpreted
for them the things concerning himself in all the Scriptures.
—Luke 24:27

For many years, I read the different books of the Bible as if they were
disconnected from the whole. In my reading plan during my teenage
and college years, I would pick a book from either the Old Testament or
the New, and begin to read, take notes, and pray over what I read. While
the first step to understanding the Bible begins with reading, I found that
my perception of God's Word sharpened when I was introduced to the
concept of biblical theology. I learned through studies in seminary, as well
as through my local church, that the Bible has an overarching storyline,
and each book of the Bible should be read and interpreted in light of
that particular book's place within the canon of Scripture. The Bible has
a unified message, and understanding that message is the key to rightly
interpreting and teaching the texts of Scripture.

The first chapter defined and discussed the nature of the Bible, highlighting that God has spoken to his people through general revelation
(that of creation) and through special revelation (the Scriptures). The core
characteristics of the Bible (inspired, inerrant, infallible, authoritative,

necessary, sufficient, and clear) were introduced as markers each teacher of the Bible should consider as she develops her understanding and doctrine of the Word. This chapter will introduce another characteristic of the Bible: its unity and Christotelic storyline, presenting the concept of biblical theology (promoting an understanding of the metanarrative of the Scriptures). You will be trained to connect a text to the metanarrative and to Christ and the gospel.

The Unity of the Bible

Many theologians and professors repeat the adage that the Bible contains 66 books written by 40 different authors over the span of 1,500 years. To put this truth into perspective, at the time of this writing, 1,500 years ago was the year 521 AD. Imagine all that has taken place during those 1500 years until today: the Middle Ages, the Renaissance, the Reformation, the Enlightenment, the Industrial Revolution, and on until post-modern times. With that span of history in mind, consider that a period of 1,500 years to write the entirety of the Bible is an extremely consequential amount of time.

Not only was the Bible written spanning centuries, but it was written by numerous writers from various backgrounds, with different giftings and callings. The Bible contains historical books written by Moses and prophetic literature written by prophets like Isaiah, Jeremiah, Ezekiel, and Daniel. It encompasses poetry, songs, and wisdom writings penned by people like David and Solomon, as well as historical books which were anonymously written. It contains the Gospels and Epistles, written by the apostles, as well as apocalyptic texts written by Daniel and John. When the apostle John composed the book of Revelation, typically regarded as the last book of the Bible to be written, he was as far removed in time from the writing of the book of Job (which is regarded as the first book of the Bible to be written) as readers today are removed from 521 AD. And yet, the Bible, written over a great span of time, by various people, contains a unified message: Jesus Christ and him crucified. The unity of the Bible is thus defined by James Hernando as:

The belief that the Bible presents a coherent unified perspective in its essential teachings (Ramm 1970, 174), stemming from the conviction that behind the diverse writings of Scripture there is a single divine Author (McQuilken, 21, 68–69; Terry, 383) who speaks a unified message in and throughout the biblical canon. The interpreter who adopts this presupposition will see the entire Bible, in a sense, as the literary and theological context for interpretation.[1]

Hernando's definition for biblical unity points out that an interpreter's belief in the unified message of the Bible impacts the method of interpretation employed by the Bible student. The unified message of Christ and him crucified should be further explored to aid us in our quest of faithful biblical interpretation.

The Overarching Story and Overarching Subject of Scripture

In the past decade or so, the Christian community has increasingly emphasized the need for Christ-centered teaching, preaching, and Bible study due to a pervading culture of moralism in the church. Pastors, seminary professors, and curriculum writers recognized that in the last thirty to forty years Christian morals have often been taught without connecting Christian behavior to the gospel. The impetus for godly living has not been an understanding of a believer's union with Christ that results in obedience, but rather obedience to New Testament imperative commands as a means of achieving godliness. Thus, Christian leaders have produced a plethora of books, commentaries, and sermons devoted to either a Christ-centered or gospel-centered interpretation of the Scriptures.

Since moralism has impacted Christianity in varying degrees throughout Christian history, a cohesive understanding of God's Word enables the Bible teacher to anchor all Bible teaching to Christ and his

---

[1] Hernando, *Dictionary of Hermeneutics* (see chap. 1, n. 21), 41.

story of redeeming the world. Thus, a helpful way of discerning God's plan is to ask the simple question, What is God's story? Or the question may be rephrased: *What is the overarching story* that God is conveying to us through the Bible? Another helpful question to ask is, *Who is the main character* in God's story? In his book *The Story of Scripture: An Introduction to Biblical Theology*, Matthew Y. Emerson answers both questions as he points readers to the work of Geerhardus Vos in the area of biblical theology. Biblical theology is defined as a theological discipline that "is principally concerned with the overall theological message of the whole Bible. It seeks to understand the parts in relation to the whole and, to achieve this, it must work with the mutual interaction of the literary, historical, and theological dimensions of the various corpora, and with the inter-relationships of these within the whole canon of Scripture."[2] When Emerson answers the questions posed above (what is the Bible's overarching story and who is the main character of that story), he identifies Jesus as the main character or subject of the Bible and "the grand narrative from creation (Genesis 1) to new creation (Revelation 21) as the overarching storyline of the Bible."[3] These two categories (overarching story and overarching subject) provide a foundation for a right understanding of biblical interpretation and are the lenses through which we should see all of the Bible.

A clarifying analogy may be helpful. Imagine needing glasses to see the world clearly. For some people, imagination is not required because that is their reality. However, for those who wear glasses or those who do not, consider the makeup of glasses as a beneficial illustration to understand the concepts being taught. A pair of glasses has a lens for the right eye and a lens for the left eye. The frame holds both lenses in place. When studying the Scriptures, the best frame to wear for reading and comprehending the Bible is biblical theology, and the two lenses are the overarching story and the overarching subject. When both lenses are

---

[2] T. Desmond Alexander and Brian S. Rosner, eds., *New Dictionary of Biblical Theology* (Downers Grove, IL: InterVarsity, 2000), 3.

[3] Matthew Y. Emerson, *The Story of Scripture: An Introduction to Biblical Theology* (Nashville: B&H Academic, 2017), 4.

paired, one's ability to see the meaning of specific biblical texts is sharp-ened. This concept begs two questions: What are the details of the over-arching story? And, How is Christ presented as the main subject of the Bible? The grand narrative of Scripture (also called the metanarrative or overarching storyline) articulates God's story through four markers: creation, fall, redemption, and restoration; and each marker points to Christ, the subject of the story. Genesis 1–3 provides the overall basis for this paradigm of understanding God's Word and each of the four mark-ers explored below.

Creation

In Genesis 1 and 2, the text teaches that the triune God created the world and everything in it in six days. The created order includes light (and the institution of day and night), the sky, the dry land (which he called earth), the sea, vegetation, the sun, moon, and stars, sea creatures, birds, livestock and wildlife. Finally, on the sixth day, God created man and woman in his image, and "God blessed them, and God said to them, 'Be fruitful, mul-tiply, fill the earth, and subdue it. Rule the fish of the sea, the birds of the sky, and every creature that crawls on the earth'" (Gen 1:28). While Genesis 1 provides the overall account of the six days of creation, with man and woman being created and given both a blessing and command by God, Genesis 2 provides a more detailed account of the events of the sixth day. That particular chapter gives insight into the specific features of day six where readers learn that God formed Adam, planted a garden in Eden, and placed Adam "in the garden of Eden to work it and watch over it" (Gen 2:15). The Lord tells Adam that he is free to eat of any tree in the garden except "from the tree of the knowledge of good and evil" (Gen 2:16). To this point, all of the events of day six have taken place before the woman has been created. And, everything up to that point in the creation narrative is counted by the Lord as good. A shift, however, is seen in Gen 2:18 when God comments that "it is not good" for Adam to be alone. At this moment, God creates the woman as "a helper corresponding to" Adam.

The account of the creation of the world and the creation of man and woman provides the rich knowledge of God's plan from the very beginning that is carried throughout the pages of the Bible up to present day. God created humankind to bring him glory by ruling and reigning over the world, establishing communities and culture, and to ultimately commune with him as they extend his rule over the earth.

Fall

Genesis 3 articulates the fall of man and woman into sin as well as the consequences for sin. The well-known text tells the story of the serpent and the woman, and how the serpent tricks the woman into disbelieving the goodness of both God and his commands. The serpent's deception results in the woman taking the forbidden fruit, eating it, and giving it to Adam, who eats it as well, plunging himself and all humanity into a state of sin resulting in death (vv. 1–7). Thus, Genesis 1–3 is the foundation for biblical anthropology: men and women are created in the image of God to commune with him and extend his rule, but now exist in a state of fallenness, separated from God and dead in their sin. This instance in Genesis explains the pain that humans encounter from Genesis 3 onward to today because of the consequences of sin and its effects on a broken world (vv. 8–20). As one reads throughout the Bible, the story is one tale after another of the broken relationship between God and man, and the broken relationship from one person to the next. This truth is exemplified in Genesis 4 as we witness Cain's anger toward God and his brother, resulting in the first murder in history.

Redemption

Amazingly, in the midst of God's pronouncement of judgment and curse in Genesis 3, he offers the hope of redemption. In verse 15, the Lord God tells the serpent, "I will put hostility between you and the woman, and between your offspring and her offspring. He will strike your head, and you will strike his heel." Various theologians and scholars debate the meaning of this verse with some believing the word "offspring" refers to a collective group of people who will gain victory over Satan. Others hold that the reference to a victorious offspring who strikes the head of the serpent is none other than Jesus Christ.[4] Yet others, such as Martin Luther, believed that "'her seed' [is a] reference to both humanity in general and Christ in particular."[5] The book of Hebrews and the book of Romans each help to solidify the general and particular interpretation cited by Luther. The writer of Hebrews points to Christ as the one who overcame the devil on the cross: "Now since the children have flesh and blood in common, Jesus also shared in these, so that through his death he might destroy the one holding the power of death—that is, the devil" (Heb 2:14), while the apostle Paul reminds the church at Rome, "The God of peace will soon crush Satan under your feet" (Rom 16:20).

Thus, the interpretive lens of the story of God is best understood when the Bible student is cognizant of the ongoing struggle between the people of God and those who are of the devil. Often, biblical theologians point to two genealogical lines in Genesis that reflect this struggle: the "ungodly line of Cain" found in Genesis 4 and the "godly line of Seth" found in Genesis 5. This framework allows us to understand the overarching struggle of the people of God in the Old Testament that finds ultimate fulfillment in the New Testament:

> We should observe that the righteous line of Seth plays a central role in the outworking of God's purposes for the redemption of humanity. As members of this lineage, Noah and Abraham are especially significant. Whereas the righteousness of the former prevents the whole human race from being exterminated in the flood, through Abraham and his offspring all the nations of the earth will be blessed. This divine blessing, guaranteed by oath on account of Abraham's obedience, will come through a future royal descendant (Gen. 22:16–18). Although Genesis concludes by associating future royalty with Joseph and the line of Ephraim,

---

[4] For a study of the historical interpretations of this verse, see John Calvin's *Commentary on the Book of Genesis*, *The New American Commentary on Genesis 1–11:26* by Kenneth A. Mathews, and *From Eden to New Jerusalem: An Introduction to Biblical Theology* by T. Desmond Alexander.

[5] Kenneth A. Mathews, *The New American Commentary on Genesis 1–11:26* (Nashville: B&H Publishing, 1996), 247.

the expectation is introduced that in time kingship will come through the tribe of Judah and the descendants of David.[6]

The hope of redemption offered in Gen 3:15 hints at the unfolding drama of human history seen in the pages of the Old Testament, pointing to not only the overarching story of God but also the overarching subject: Jesus and his victory over Satan.

While the Lord had cursed the serpent (v. 14), announced the consequences for sin upon both Adam (vv. 17–19) and the woman (v. 16), and prophesied the hope of redemption in Gen 3:15, atonement for sin was needed for Adam and his wife. They had both disobeyed God by falling prey to the temptations of the serpent, and verse 7 teaches that "the eyes of both of them were opened, and they knew they were naked; so they sewed fig leaves together and made coverings for themselves." Verses 8–10 reveal that Adam and the woman hid from God and were afraid. Sadly, Adam and his wife began to shift the blame when God confronted them about their sinful actions (vv. 11–13). These verses highlight how sin fragmented the relationship between God and humankind, and between Adam and the woman, and their specific need of redemption.

Whereas the first half of Genesis 3 reveals the sad consequences and devastating effects of sin, the last half of the chapter reveals the grace of God as he takes the initiative to redeem the broken relationship that existed between the human couple and himself because of their sin. Verse 21 foreshadows how God would accomplish redemption through his Son—through an atoning sacrifice for sin. The text tells us that "the Lord God made clothing from skins for the man and his wife, and he clothed them." Adam and the woman had tried to cover themselves by sewing fig leaves together (v. 7) but God provided a better covering than they could ever devise. In their commentary on Genesis, Allen Ross and John Oswalt show that verse 21 exemplifies God's grace as he "delivered the man and the woman from living in this state of guilty fear" by

---

[6] T. Desmond Alexander, *From Eden to New Jerusalem: An Introduction to Biblical Theology* (Grand Rapids: Kregel Academic, 2008), 108–9.

providing animal skins for their covering. They note that "nothing is said of the animals or how this was done," but point to Genesis 4 where "Abel knows how to bring an animal sacrifice to God." They also argue that "the Israelite reader would think of sacrifice, as well, because in the Tabernacle the skins of the animals went to the priests for clothing," ultimately concluding that "God was not satisfied that a bunch of leaves snatched from a tree would cover the sinners' guilty fears. No, because of the seriousness of sin, a life would be relinquished instead (Ezek 18:20; Rom 6:23)."[7] Thus, the covering with animal skin in Gen 3:21 hinted at the need for a substitute and revealed God's redemption of sinners from death to new life.

While God provided redemption for Adam and his wife in verse 21, the woman is renamed in verse 20, signifying the hope Adam had in the promise God gave to the serpent in Gen 3:15 (that the offspring of the woman would crush the head of the serpent). Genesis 3:20 says, "The man named his wife Eve because she was the mother of all the living." Initially, Adam had named his wife "woman" (2:23), signifying both their sameness and distinctiveness (scholars often note how the Hebrew word for man and woman sound similar). Yet, in Gen 3:20, the narrative teaches that Adam gives the woman a new name (Eve, meaning "life") that reflects the salvific promise of God. Both man and woman had transgressed and brought death into the world, yet from verse 20 onward, when Adam and Eve spoke or heard her new name, they would forever be reminded of the promised One to come who would bring victory over the sin and death they introduced into the world. The Lord had covered the sin of Adam and Eve and assured victory to come through the promised offspring. In naming Eve, Adam made sure that neither he nor Eve would ever forget that promise. And with that promise and new name comes the hope that Adam and Eve would be restored to their original purpose: to be fruitful, multiply, fill the whole earth, and subdue it (Gen 1:28).

---

[7] Allen P. Ross and John N. Oswalt, *Genesis, Exodus* (CBC) (Carol Stream, IL: Tyndale House, 2008), 57.

Restoration

While Adam and Eve had been promised redemption and given the hope of restoration, they were not yet completely restored, evidenced by the concluding verses in Genesis 3: "So the Lord God sent him away from the garden of Eden to work the ground from which he was taken. He drove the man out and stationed the cherubim and the flaming, whirling sword east of the garden of Eden to guard the way to the tree of life." The command that Adam disobeyed was eating from "the tree of knowledge of good and evil" (2:17), resulting in Adam becoming like God, knowing good and evil. Consequently, the Lord banished Adam and Eve from Eden so that they would not "reach out, take from the tree of life, eat, and live forever" (3:22). At this juncture, Adam and Eve, though possibly redeemed, still existed in a fallen state and under God's judgment, will die (3:19). The Lord prevented Adam and Eve from living eternally in their fallen state by expelling them from the garden. This series of events lead to the continued story of God's people longing to return to God's garden, living in fellowship and under the blessing of God's rule.[8] Genesis 3 concludes with man being driven out and leaves us longing for restoration of man's first state when he was in unhindered, unbroken, sin-free fellowship with God.

Thus, the pattern of creation, fall, redemption, and restoration seen in Genesis 1–3 is the overarching story that shapes the entirety of the Bible. It provides a narrative pattern that is furthered and expanded as the Bible progresses. Genesis 1–3 is a microcosm of the greater storyline that takes shape from Genesis to Revelation, as reflected in the table below. Column one lists the four markers of the biblical storyline (creation, fall, redemption, restoration), while column two illustrates Genesis 1–3. Finally, in the third column, the table reflects the movement of the story toward redemption and restoration, where hints of redemption and restoration are longed for and sometimes found. As the table underscores in column

---

[8] Graeme Goldsworthy, *Gospel and Kingdom* (Crownhill, UK: Paternoster, 1981), 54–55.

three, redemption is fully realized with the incarnation of Christ and restoration is realized with the return of Christ.

Overarching Story	Genesis 1–3	Biblical Pattern
Creation	Adam and the Woman created in God's image to be fruitful, multiply, fill the whole earth, and subdue it (Gen 1:28).	The descendants of Adam and his wife, throughout the Old and New Testament, are fruitful, multiply, fill the earth, and subdue it. They cultivate the land, establish families, build cities and cultures, and exercise dominion over animals.
Fall	Adam and the Woman transgress God's Word and fall into sin (Gen 3:1–7).	The descendants of Adam and Eve (all of humankind) inherit a sinful nature that is reflected by their dishonoring of God and his commands. They fail to worship him as the One True God and worship and serve creation instead (Rom 1:18–25).
Redemption	God curses the serpent and promises that there will be enmity between the offspring of the serpent and the offspring of the woman, yet the offspring of the woman will crush the head of the serpent (Gen 3:15).	The descendants of Adam and Eve begin to reflect the offspring of the woman or the offspring of the serpent, echoed in the godly line of Seth (Gen 4:25–5:32) or the wicked line of Cain (Gen 4:15–24).

Redemption (*cont.*)		Noah, born of the line of Seth, is hoped to be the offspring who would bring relief from the curse (Gen 5:29), is righteous and blameless (Gen 6:9), obeys God's command, and saves his family from God's flood of judgment (Genesis 6–8).
		Abram is called out by the Lord to a specific land, is given the promise that he will be made into a great nation and that all the peoples of the earth would be blessed through him. (Gen 12:1–2). As Abram hopes in these promises, God promises further that Abram's offspring would be as numerous as the stars (Gen 15:1–5). Abraham and Sarah, counted as though dead, receive the power to conceive Isaac, and through Isaac and Jacob are blessed with offspring as numerous as the stars and sand. Abraham's great-grandsons form the twelve tribes of Israel. A king from the tribe of Judah is prophesied (Gen 49:9–10).
		Moses acts as a prophet who speaks for God, redeeming Israel from the slavery of Egypt. Moses is used by God to give Israel the Law, and he prophesies of a greater prophet to come (Deut 18:15).

Redemption (*cont.*)		Joshua is appointed by the Lord to succeed Moses and leads the Israelites into conquest to obtain the Promised Land, allotting the land for each tribe, minus the tribe of Levi, which was given cities instead of territories (Joshua 1–21). Thus, "None of the good promises the LORD had made to the house of Israel failed. Everything was fulfilled" (Josh 21:45).
		David lives in the Promised Land and rules over Israel as king but his reign is fraught with sin and family discord. David is promised an offspring who will rule on his throne for eternity, establishing God's kingdom and building a house for God's name (2 Sam 7:11–14a).
		Isaiah prophesies that a child will be born and the government will rest on his shoulders, whose dominion will be vast, who will reign on the throne of David, and who is named Mighty God, Eternal Father, Prince of Peace (Isa 9:6–7). This child is also the suffering servant who is pierced and crushed for his people's iniquities (Isaiah 53).

Redemption (*cont.*)		The second person of the Trinity, the Son, takes on flesh. Jesus Christ crushes the head of the serpent in his work upon the cross and redeems God's people from their sin. Jesus is the promised offspring, the Israel of God (Gal 3:16) so that every promise of God finds its yes and amen in Christ (2 Cor 1:20).
		The church is promised that God will soon crush Satan under its feet (Rom 16:20) and that she will conquer him by the blood of the lamb and the word of her testimony (Rev 12:11).
		At the end, the dragon (the ancient serpent) and the beast wage war on the offspring of the woman/saints (Rev 12:9, 13–17; 13:5–8).
		The beast, the kings of the earth, and their armies gather to wage war on Jesus, but are destroyed by the sword coming from the mouth of Christ (Rev 19:11–21).

Restoration	Adam and Eve are banished from the garden of Eden, leading to hopeful longing among God's people for a return to God's garden, living in fellowship with him under his rule.	After the flood, Noah is given the command to be fruitful, multiply, and fill the earth (Gen 9:1, 7) and God makes a covenant with Noah to never again destroy the earth with a flood.

Abraham looks forward to the city whose builder is God (Heb 11:8–12).

Before his death, the Lord shows Moses the land promised to Abraham, Isaac, and Jacob, and promises Moses he will give the land to all his descendants. Yet, the Lord does not allow Moses to cross over into the land; Moses dies and is buried in the land of Moab (Deut 34:1–6).

Before his death, Joshua reminds the Israelites of all the Lord has done to bring them into the Promised Land and renews God's covenant with them for blessing in the land. Yet, Israel is promised that if they fail to drive out the conquered nations and tear down the altars to their false gods, the people and their gods will be a trap for Israel (Joshua 23–Judges). |

Restoration (*cont.*)		David sins against God and neighbor by committing adultery and murder; he humbly repents and confesses his sin, praying for personal restoration, as well as for the good of the kingdom. He asks God to cause Zion to prosper and to build the walls of Jerusalem (2 Sam 11–12; Psalm 51).
		Isaiah prophesies about the restoration of Zion, speaking of Jerusalem as a land of delight in which the Lord will establish the city as a place inhabited by holy people, the redeemed, who are cared for and never deserted (Isa 49:8; 62). Isaiah further prophesies about the creation of a new heaven and a new earth, where Jerusalem will be a place of joy, where people will build houses and plant vineyards, and where God's offspring will remain forever (Isaiah 65–66).
		Jesus promises to return and will have his angels gather his people from the four corners of the earth (Matt 24:31).

| Restoration (*cont.*) | | As the church awaits the return of Christ, she is promised the presence of Christ as she obeys his commission to go and make disciples of all nations (Matt 28:16–20). She is reminded that on earth she has no enduring city but is to seek the city to come (Heb 13:14). |
| | | At the end, after anyone whose name is not found in the Lamb's book of life is cast into the lake of fire, the New Jerusalem will come down out of heaven from God, and God will dwell with humanity. He will make all things new. The nations will walk in the light of the glory of God, and the glory and honor of the nations will be brought into the city. The tree of life will be accessible to all who enter: its leaves will heal the nations and there will no longer be any curse (Revelation 21–22). |

When one reads the Bible, no matter the text, they must understand how the text fits the whole in relation to what God is doing in redemptive history. Therefore, an understanding of the overarching story (creation, fall, redemption, and restoration) and the overarching subject (Jesus Christ) will enable one to connect a text within the storyline and to Christ.

Connecting a Text to the Storyline and to Christ

The section and table above outlined the major storyline of the Bible using the four markers of creation, fall, redemption, and restoration. The table reveals the pattern of Genesis 1–3, and how the themes in the first few chapters of Genesis are further expanded throughout the Old and New Testaments. However, when looking at a particular text, the connection a text may have to the overall message of the Bible and to Christ may be unclear for a Bible student. Therefore, take the following steps to connect a text to the storyline and to Christ by reading a particular text with the following questions in mind:

1. What elements or hints of creation are found in the passage?
2. How does the passage reveal the fallenness of humankind?
3. How does the passage display the struggle between the offspring of the woman and the offspring of the serpent? Does the passage incorporate a person who may foreshadow Christ by redeeming or rescuing God's people?
4. How does the passage convey the restoration of God's people? If it does not give details about immediate restoration in the context, how does it cause longing for the complete restoration of God's people in Revelation 21–22?

The following example from Judges 6 illustrates how to connect a particular text to the overall story and subject of the Bible by answering each of the four questions above. Take a moment to read Judg 6:1–10 (at least 2–3 times) and then answer the questions above before continuing. Once you have answered the four questions, you may want to review my answers to the questions, below.

1. What elements or hints of creation are found in the passage?

   Israel has been given the Promised Land where, ideally, they are to fulfill the creation mandate given to Adam and Eve: to be fruitful, multiply, fill the earth, and subdue it. They are to cultivate the land, establish families, build cities and cultures, and exercise dominion over animals.

2.   How does the passage reveal the fallenness of humankind?

Judges 6:1–6 says, "The Israelites did what was evil in the sight of the Lord. So the Lord handed them over to Midian seven years, and they oppressed Israel. Because of Midian, the Israelites made hiding places for themselves in the mountains, caves, and strongholds. Whenever the Israelites planted crops, the Midianites, Amalekites, and the people of the east came and attacked them. They encamped against them and destroyed the produce of the land, even as far as Gaza. They left nothing for Israel to eat, as well as no sheep, ox, or donkey. For the Midianites came with their cattle and their tents like a great swarm of locusts. They and their camels were without number, and they entered the land to lay waste to it. So Israel became poverty-stricken because of Midian, and the Israelites cried out to the Lord."

The passage reveals the fallenness of humankind in three ways:

a) A broken relationship with God—Israel does what is evil in the sight of the Lord (while this passage does outline the specific sin they commit, the phrase "did what was evil in the sight of the Lord" is also mentioned in Judg 2:11 and 3:7). A quick look at the cross-references for 6:1 reveals that both 2:11 and 3:7 state the evil outright: they worship the Baals and abandon the Lord. The evil Israel commits in Judges 6 is a continued pattern of worshiping idols and turning away from Yahweh, the One True God.

b) A broken relationship with neighbors—Midian oppresses Israel for seven years, and the Israelites are attacked by Midianites, Amalekites, and people from the east.

c) The effects of living in a fallen world—Instead of experiencing the goodness of the Promised Land (a land flowing with milk and honey, which was to be a blessing to God's people like the garden of Eden), Israel is left with nothing to eat because their enemies destroy the produce. The Midianites "lay waste" to the land, resulting in poverty and despair for Israel.

3. How does the passage display the struggle between the offspring
    of the woman and the offspring of the serpent? Does the passage
    incorporate a person who may foreshadow Christ by redeeming
    or rescuing God's people?

    The passage displays a struggle between Israel and the
    Midianites. The Midianites oppress Israel, and are used by God
    to draw Israel to repentance (Judg 6:1–2, 7). The Lord sends a
    prophet to remind Israel that they were redeemed by God when
    he brought them out of Egypt and "out of the place of slavery"
    (6:8–9). The prophet in the passage points to Christ, who is the
    true and greater Prophet (Acts 3:22–23).

    This particular passage (Judg 6:1–10) does not illustrate redemp-
    tion but Gideon is used by God in the following verses/chapters
    to rescue God's people from the Midianites (8:22, 28).

4. How does the passage convey the restoration of God's people? If
    it does not give details about immediate restoration in the con-
    text, how does it cause longing for the complete restoration of
    God's people in Revelation 21–22?

    In Judg 6:10, the prophet tells the people that the Lord said
    to them, "I am the LORD your God. Do not fear the gods of
    the Amorites whose land you live in. But you did not obey
    me." Thus, Judg 6:1–10 does not convey that the people are
    restored but reminds us that the Israelites did not obey the
    Lord's consistent warning not to worship other gods. The
    actions of the Israelites, who fail to honor God by remem-
    bering how he rescued them from Egypt and redeemed their
    lives from slavery, and who turn to worship false idols, causes
    us to long for the time when God's people will worship him
    alone, free from wicked hearts that turn to idolatry—which
    ultimately occurs in Christ.

For Further Study and Practice

Readers are encouraged to grow in their understanding of the unity of the Bible by studying the concept of biblical theology. The following books are recommended:

- *From Eden to the New Jerusalem: An Introduction to Biblical Theology* by T. Desmond Alexander
- *The Story of Scripture: An Introduction to Biblical Theology* by Matthew Y. Emerson
- *God's Big Picture: Tracing the Storyline of the Bible* by Vaughan Roberts

Readers should also practice connecting various Bible texts (from both the Old and New Testaments) to the overall story and subject of the Bible by answering each of the four questions provided.

3

The Genres of the Bible

I have your decrees as a heritage forever; indeed, they are the joy
of my heart. I am resolved to obey your statutes to the very end.
—Psalm 119:111–112

While the Bible is unified in its theme and subject, the book contains
various forms of literature to convey its overall message. As noted in
chapter 2, the Bible contains 66 books written by 40 different authors,
over the span of 1,500 years. If God is a creative God, and not only the
natural world, but the people made in God's image reflect his imaginative
and artistic character, then so the Bible, penned by human authors under
the inspiration of the Spirit, reflects his artistic, imaginative nature. Thus,
the human authors of the Bible reflect the character of God when they
employ different kinds of writing and literature to speak and teach truth
through the written word. Every single one of the human authors was
used by God, with their distinct personalities, to write exactly what the
Holy Spirit intended, through the forms the different writers used. The
Bible fully displays humanity's proclivity for artistic expression, bringing
glory to a creative God through the art of literature.

This chapter will discuss the various genres found within the
Bible (narrative, law, poetry, wisdom, prophecy, gospels, epistles, and

apocalyptic), equipping you to better comprehend, interpret, and teach the Scriptures. Often, Christians mistakenly interpret all biblical passages according to the method used to discern the epistles. Yet, the various genres of the Bible demand that you approach each type of text with its genre in mind, preventing a misinterpretation of the text's purpose. The chapter will consider each biblical genre below and will provide interpretive help according to each genre.

Narrative

While the Bible contains many forms of literature, narratives make up the majority of the Scriptures. Biblical narratives are historically accurate accounts of how God worked in the lives of his people in both the Old and New Testaments. One may read a historical story recorded in the Old Testament and wonder how the events that took place thousands of years ago in the lives of people like Ruth, Esther, or David are relevant in modern times. The apostle Paul clarifies why biblical narratives are needed. In writing to the church at Corinth, he reflects on the disobedience of the Israelites after Moses led them out of Egypt, and reminds the Corinthian Christians that God preserved those stories to be instructive for them as they follow Christ (1 Cor 10:1–13). While 1 Corinthians 10 is speaking explicitly about the story of Moses and the people of God being led out of slavery, an implication of Paul's words—that the Scriptures were written for Christian instruction—is that the entirety of the Old Testament narratives provides wisdom and instruction for the Christian life. Thus, Bible students must know the stories of the Bible and how to adequately discern the instruction God wants to convey.

The following books are either all narrative or contain narrative accounts within them: Genesis, Exodus, Numbers, Deuteronomy, Joshua, Judges, Ruth, 1 and 2 Samuel, 1 and 2 Kings, 1 and 2 Chronicles, Ezra, Nehemiah, Esther, Job, Isaiah, Jeremiah, Ezekiel, Daniel, Jonah, Haggai, the Gospels, and Acts. Since the majority of the narratives derive from the Old Testament, this section will consider elements pertinent to those found within the Old Testament, but application may be made to narrative accounts found within the New Testament.

Gordon Fee and Douglas Stuart highlight the "three levels" of an Old Testament narrative in their book, *How to Read the Bible for All Its Worth*. These three levels are illustrated below.

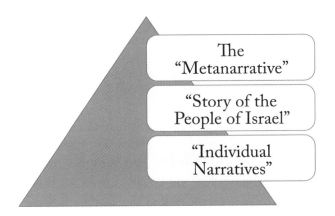

Individual narratives are the basic accounts that are found within the Old Testament which contribute to the larger story that the Bible is telling (in the Old Testament, the "story of the people of Israel") and the overall metanarrative (see chap. 2) from Genesis to Revelation.[1] When studying a biblical narrative, you should consider the individual narrative, its relationship to the story of the people of Israel, and the location of the narrative within the larger context of the Bible's overarching story.

To better discern the meaning of the story, readers should identify the main elements of individual narratives: (1) the plot, (2) the characters, and (3) the setting. The plot consists of elements such as conflict (some type of struggle in need of resolution), suspense (the question of what will cause the conflict to be resolved), peripetia (an unexpected turn of events), and the denouement (the point of conflict resolution). Regarding characters, the actors contained within stories are often grouped into one of three categories: "The 'protagonist' (the primary person in the story), the 'antagonist' (the person who brings about the conflict or tension), and (sometimes) the 'agonist(s)' (the other major characters in the story who

---

[1] Gordon D. Fee and Douglas Stuart, *How to Read the Bible for All Its Worth*, 3rd ed. (Grand Rapids: Zondervan, 2003), 90–91.

get involved in the struggle)."[2] The setting consists of location and time in which the story takes place.

The three levels and the three main elements of an Old Testament narrative both provide the main aids to understand biblical stories. As readers identify the three levels and three main elements of any narrative, they will have greater discernment in understanding the meaning of the text (see chapters 4, 5, and 6).

Law

The classical sense of the term *law*, when used in reference to the Bible, denotes the first five books of the Old Testament but can refer to many elements of the Scriptures. Fee and Douglas provide a helpful list of all that could be meant by the term, noting that its typical usage is

1. in the plural to refer to the "laws"—those 600-plus specific commands that the Israelites were expected to keep as evidence of their loyalty to God (e.g., Ex 18:20);
2. in the singular to refer to all of these laws collectively (e.g., Matt 5:18);
3. in the singular to refer to the Pentateuch (Genesis to Deuteronomy) as the "Book of the Law" (e.g., Josh 1:8);
4. in the singular by some writers in the New Testament to refer theologically to the entire Old Testament religious system (e.g., 1 Cor 9:20);
5. in the singular by some New Testament personages to refer to the Old Testament law (in sense 2 above) as it was interpreted by the rabbis (e.g., Peter in Acts 10:28).[3]

When seeking to understand the biblical genre of the law, each of the five uses above may be referenced in the section that follows.

If one were to enter a discussion with believers concerning Old Testament law, the conversation would likely entertain the question,

---

[2] Fee and Stuart, 90.

[3] Fee and Stuart, 164.

"Does the law apply to Christians today?" This question, at its heart, is seeking to determine the relevance and binding nature that the Old Testament law may or may not have upon Christians. Interestingly, one's theological system influences the way they answer the question and the way they interpret the law in the Bible. Their answer to the question and their interpretive method of Old Testament law likely stems from the theological system they have studied or been influenced by. For example, those impacted by dispensational theology may answer the question that neither Old Testament law nor the Sermon on the Mount apply to believers today. Yet, some dispensationalists may believe that the moral aspects of the Mosaic law or Sermon on the Mount apply in some way to Christians.

For others who may be influenced by a more covenantal approach to the Bible, the answer to the question of the law's application to believers may vary. Covenant theologians often use the "tripartite division" of the Mosaic law to determine which portions Christians are obligated to keep. The tripartite division understands the Mosaic law as: 1) civil—governmental laws for the nation of Israel; 2) ceremonial—the laws given to the nation of Israel that pertain to the sacrificial system and other ceremonies; and 3) moral—ethical regulations for Israel, summarized in the Ten Commandments. They would conclude that the civil and ceremonial laws do not apply because Christ fulfilled those laws, but would understand the moral law as binding, including keeping the Sabbath.

Covenant theologians often appeal to the "three-fold office and use of the moral law" as outlined by Calvin in his book, *Institutes of the Christian Religion*: 1) as a mirror (to reveal personal sin and its consequences), 2) as a curb (to prevent sin and maintain order); and 3) as a guide (to point toward godly living).[4] Others, working from a covenantal framework known as "Progressive Covenantalism," emphasize the entire Scripture as authoritative and dislike the use of the tripartite division to determine the binding nature of the moral law, since the Scriptures themselves do

---

[4] John Calvin, *Institutes of the Christian Religion*, trans. Henry Beveridge (Peabody, MA: Hendrickson, 2009), 222–26.

not appeal to such a division of the law. Instead, they would interpret the entirety of Old Testament law as fulfilled by Christ.[5]

The covenantal frameworks (though they vary) present aspects that will aid the Bible student who desires to understand and apply Old Testament law to the Christian. First and foremost, Christ should be seen as the fulfillment of Old Testament law, whether the laws are dealing with Israel civically, ceremonially, or morally. The New Testament teaches that "Christ is the end of the law for righteousness to everyone who believes" (Rom 10:4). The particular point to remember is that Christ is the goal or aim of the law. Thus, Jesus said, "Don't think that I came to abolish the Law or the Prophets. I did not come to abolish but to fulfill" (Matt 5:17). Jesus is proclaiming that he is the fulfillment of the Old Testament in toto, and as such, "all of the Old Testament remains normative and relevant for Jesus's followers (2 Tim. 3:16), but none of it can rightly be interpreted until one understands how it has been fulfilled in Christ. Every Old Testament text must be viewed in light of Jesus's person and ministry and the changes introduced by the new covenant he inaugurated."[6]

Second, readers are encouraged to consider the principle being communicated through the law because

> God intends [the law] to serve as a paradigm of timeless ethical, moral, and theological principles. . . . The law is more than a temporary, dispensable cultural phenomenon. Actually, it plays a key role in Israel's priestly ministry as a "light to the nations" . . . Christians who dismiss it as outmoded and irrelevant deprive themselves of the teachings God conveyed through it. They miss an additional resource for understanding what it might mean to be Christ-like.[7]

---

[5] For a summary discussion on the relationship between one's theological system and the interpretation of Old Testament law, see Benjamin L. Merkle, *Discontinuity to Continuity: A Survey of Dispensational and Covenantal Theologies* (Bellingham, WA: Lexham, 2020), 203, 205–6, 208, 210.

[6] Craig L. Blomberg, *New American Commentary: Matthew*, vol. 22 (Nashville: Broadman, 1992), 104.

[7] William W. Klein, Craig L. Blomberg, and Robert L. Hubbard Jr., *Introduction to Biblical Interpretation*, 3rd ed. (Grand Rapids: Zondervan Academic, 2017), 444.

For example, a reader may be overwhelmed with the rules and regulations presented in a book of the law like Leviticus, with its purification rituals and laws about cleansing. Yet, the enduring theological principle of such laws reminds Christians today about the holiness of God and their own need for cleansing by Christ before being brought near to God.

Poetry

The creativity of both God and the human authors of the Bible is majestically displayed in the genre of poetry found within biblical books such as Job, Psalms, Proverbs, Ecclesiastes, Song of Songs, and Lamentations. The poetry of the Bible pushes us to the heights of God's love, the depths of personal sin, the joy of walking closely with the Lord, and the awesome realization of the holiness and character of God. Consider the use of poetic language to convey God's power over the sea in Job 38:8–11, when the Lord answers Job,

> "Who enclosed the sea behind doors when it burst from the womb, when I made the clouds its garment and total darkness its blanket, when I determined its boundaries and put its bars and doors in place, when I declared, 'You may come this far, but no farther; your proud waves stop here'?"

Contemplate how David expresses his deep longing for the Lord when he prays to God in Ps 63:1–2,

> God, you are my God; I eagerly seek you. I thirst for you; my body faints for you in a land that is dry, desolate, and without water. So I gaze on you in the sanctuary to see your strength and your glory.

Or let the writer of Ecclesiastes move your heart to recognize the vanity of life, when he concludes that

> youth and the prime of life are fleeting. So remember your Creator in the days of your youth: Before the days of adversity come, and the years approach when you will say, "I have no delight in them." (Eccl 11:10–12:1)

Surely, the poetry of the Bible moves and stirs the heart, connecting us to the experiences of believers who have come before us, delighting us with the expression of human emotion, in turn enabling us to express what it feels like to know and walk with the God of the universe. Thus, the reason for biblical poetry rests upon its emotional import, as the *Evangelical Dictionary of Biblical Theology* concludes:

> Of paramount importance is the emotional quality inherent in poetry. Although one must recognize that prose is not devoid of emotional content, poetry conveys feelings with singular effect. In the prophetic oracle of judgment, the reader senses the fury of God's wrath, effectively communicating nuances of God's emotions ranging from cajolery to sarcasm. With love poetry such as the Song of Solomon, lovers express much of the deep emotions they hold for each other. Poetry serves the psalmist with equal dexterity as he expresses lament, praise, or thanksgiving. From complaints concerning the tardiness of God's salvation to hymns extolling the Lord's great acts of salvation, poetry conveys the deepest emotions of the author.[8]

The question arises then: What constitutes biblical poetry? Other books of the Bible contain poetry, in addition to the books named above, indicating that Bible students should be skilled in identifying poetry contained in books that contain mainly prose.[9] One must be able to determine the differences in the two because prose is to be taken in a more literal fashion, whereas poetry employs rhetorical devices like metaphor, simile, and hyperbole. Elwell points out that "there are basically two schools of literary thought on how to identify poetry. One approach attempts to make the matter purely subjective, arguing that if a text 'feels' poetic and impresses itself upon the mind of the reader as such, then

---

[8] Walter A. Elwell, ed., *Evangelical Dictionary of Biblical Theology* (Grand Rapids: Baker Academic, 1996), 616.

[9] Prose is defined as "written language in its ordinary form rather than poetry." *Cambridge Dictionary*, https://dictionary.cambridge.org/us/dictionary/english/prose, accessed August 4, 2021.

the text is indeed poetic. The other school analyzes texts for diagnostic features that could delimit a passage as poetry."[10] The latter, to rely upon diagnostic features, helps readers to objectively discern that which the biblical authors intended to be poetic in nature.

English Bible translations employ a simple diagnostic feature. Stein highlights that translations delineate poetry from prose by presenting prose in paragraph form within the text and presenting poetry in broken lines of text. He presents Exodus 14–15 and Judges 4–5 as examples that contain prose (Exodus 14, Judges 4) followed by poetry (Exodus 15, Judges 5). Both instances indicate that at times biblical writers include narrative accounts written in prose followed by poetic expressions to emphasize what has taken place in the prose account. Thus, for example, Stein concludes that Judges 5 is not to be interpreted "literally, however, for this is the language of poetry. As poetry it seeks to elicit an emotive response of awe and joy rather than to impart information about the technicalities of the battle."[11]

The *Evangelical Dictionary of Biblical Theology* provides two "distinguishing features" for Hebrew poetry: the use of figurative language and the use of parallelism. First, figurative language is that which should not be taken literally. The test for determining figurative language is simple: the reader must ask of the text, "Does this text make sense in its normal sense?" If it does not, readers should seek to understand the depth of meaning behind the figures of speech. The second feature of Hebrew poetry is parallelism, which happens when "two (or sometimes more) lines are paired in such a fashion that the meaning of one line relates to the meaning of the other line(s) in one of several predictable ways."[12] Often, parallelism is employed to strengthen the meaning of one line of text by restating a truth uniquely and emphatically in the second line.

Other books containing poetry are deemed "wisdom literature" and include Job, Proverbs, and Ecclesiastes, and some of the Psalms. The first

---

[10] Elwell, *Evangelical Dictionary of Biblical Theology*, 614.

[11] Robert H. Stein, *A Basic Guide to Interpreting the Bible: Playing by the Rules*, 2nd ed. (Grand Rapids: Baker Academic, 2011), 103.

[12] Elwell, *Evangelical Dictionary of Biblical Theology*, 615.

chapter of Proverbs states the book's purpose, underlining the purpose of wisdom literature in general:

> For learning wisdom and discipline;
> for understanding insightful sayings;
> for receiving prudent instruction
> in righteousness, justice, and integrity;
> for teaching shrewdness to the inexperienced,
> knowledge and discretion to a young man. (Prov 1:2–4)

Readers may identify several aspects when reading the selection from Proverbs above. First, the format indicates that it is poetry and not prose, since it is presented in broken lines of text. Second, parallelism is used to emphasize that the proverbs have been written with the intent of teaching wisdom, discipline, understanding, instruction, shrewdness, knowledge, and discretion. The teaching then is wisdom for life and godly living.

While Job is designated as wisdom literature, it is helpful to understand that the wisdom of the book is presented to the reader in narrative form. Readers must understand the book of Job as presenting an overarching truth about human suffering through the story of Job's life. Therefore, Bible students can weave their understanding of narratives (with a plot, characters—protagonist, antagonist, and agonist(s)—and a setting) with that of poetry (the majority of dialogue presented in the book is in the form of poetry). Concerning Ecclesiastes, the *ESV Study Bible* offers a helpful list of interpretive keys:

> Many of the difficulties or paradoxes in the book can be reasonably explained in terms of: (1) his [the Preacher's] provocative style; (2) the general method of wisdom teaching, which can state apparently contradictory principles (e.g., Prov. 26:4–5) and leave it to the listener to work out which principle applies in a particular situation; and (3) the fact that, rather than focusing primarily on stating general truths that are applicable to most situations (as is the tendency with the teaching of the book of Proverbs), the Preacher devotes much of his attention to examining unique individual situations (e.g., Eccles. 4:7–8; 5:13–14;

9:13–16), which can represent deviations from what one might normally expect (e.g., 4:13–16; 9:11). Thus, while he does not deny the validity of the general depiction of reality found in the Wisdom Literature, the Preacher is also keenly aware of the complexities of life in a fallen world, which result in many individual exceptions to the "rules" of biblical wisdom.[13]

Prophecy

The books of the Bible that contain prophecy are divided into two groups: major and minor. The major prophetic books include Isaiah, Jeremiah, Lamentations, Ezekiel, and Daniel. The minor prophets include Hosea, Joel, Amos, Obadiah, Jonah, Micah, Nahum, Habakkuk, Zephaniah, Haggai, Zechariah, and Malachi. The classification of one book as a "major prophet" and another as a "minor prophet" is dependent upon the book's size, rather than level of importance. To understand the function of both major and minor prophetic books, one must be aware of the history of the nation of Israel, drawing the reader back to the need for understanding the "story of the people of Israel" as well as the metanarrative of Scripture. Walter Elwell describes the place of prophecy in relation to God's work in the lives of the nation of Israel:

> When Israel grievously strayed into idolatry, God sent prophets to announce his plans for his people. Though their proclamation often produced "foretelling" (i.e., predictions about the future), its main staple was "forthtelling" (announcements of imminent divine judgement in the present or near future). Today we read their proclamations in the books of the OT prophets, the written record of their words and deeds, a record that reflects the great rhetorical and literary creativity of both the prophets themselves and the disciples who compiled them.[14]

---

[13] "Introduction to the book of Ecclesiastes," *ESV Study Bible* (Wheaton, IL: Crossway, 2008), 1194.

[14] Klein, Blomberg, and Hubbard Jr., *Introduction to Biblical Interpretation*, 462.

Bible students should be aware that the prophets were used by God to speak prophetically to specific situations at a specific point in time, and the prophetic word given was often applicable to their immediate future. The main purpose was to call God's people to repentance from their sins, to return to worship God as he had commanded by loving and worshiping God and removing the practice of idol worship from their communities. With all this in mind, the specific prophecies that anchor the major and minor prophets to the New Testament and the church today are that of a suffering servant to come (Isaiah 53), the new covenant where believers are empowered to worship God rightly by the Spirit (Jeremiah 31 and Ezekiel 36), and the promise of being returned to the Promised Land to safely dwell forever (interpreted by some to be the same as the new heavens and the new earth).

Gospels

The Gospels are the place where the Bible student is introduced to the promised Messiah of Gen 3:15 and the reader is given an account from Matthew and John (both apostles who saw, lived, and walked with Jesus during his time on earth) as well as accounts from Mark (an attendant of the apostle Peter) and Luke (a friend who traveled with the apostle Paul, who interviewed many witnesses of Jesus's earthly ministry). Thus, these four books provide four different vantage points of eyewitness accounts that teach the reader about the life of Christ as well as substantiating Jesus as the Messiah based upon the testimony of two or more witnesses (John 8:17). The apostle John states about his Gospel, "But these things are written so that you may believe that Jesus is the Messiah, the Son of God and that by believing you may have life in his name" (John 20:31). While this verse specifically applies to the book of John, it could be said that each of the Gospels have been given so that people of all ages would believe in Jesus, the Messiah, the Son of God.

Since the Gospels offer the story of God's Son, the makeup of each book consists of narrative accounts accompanied by the teachings and sayings of Jesus (which often include parables). Readers can apply the concepts written above under "narratives" and identify the plot, the characters, and the setting for interpretive help. Concerning parables, Robert Plummer indicates that Jesus or the Gospel writer provides an interpretation or "contextual clues to the meaning of the parables" and therefore "those interpretations are definitive."[15] Consequently, when reading a parable, the Bible student should be mindful that the interpretation is often provided. Yet, if an interpretation is not given, Plummer lists five elements to help us discern the parable's meaning:

1. Determine the main point(s) of the parable—[accomplished by asking]:
   a. Who are the main characters?
   b. What occurs at the end? [Jesus often stresses his most important point at the end of a parable]
   c. What occurs in direct discourse (in quotation marks)?
   d. Who/what gets the most space?
2. Recognize stock imagery in the parables—[Plummer provides a list of stock images and their meaning/significance for the context of Jesus's day]
3. Note striking or unexpected details—[salient points are made by] striking details, unexpected twists, shocking statements, and surprise outcomes
4. Do not press all details for meaning—not all details in a parable have significance . . . many details simply make the story interesting, memorable, or true to life for the hearers
5. Pay attention to the literary and historical context of the parable—[surrounding verses indicate the reason for the parable][16]

A final word of encouragement regarding the Gospels is to remember that three of the four (Matthew, Mark, and Luke) are called the

---

[15] Robert L. Plummer, *40 Questions about Interpreting the Bible* (Grand Rapids: Kregel Academic, 2010), 266.

[16] Plummer, 273–74.

"synoptic" Gospels because they include many of the same accounts with varying degrees of information. Thus, when studying a particular passage in a Gospel account, readers may find it helpful to read the passage in conjunction with its synoptic counterpart, where they might find additional details not contained in the particular Gospel account they are studying.

Epistles

The word *epistle* literally means "letter," and the New Testament contains a few different types of letters sent from an apostle to recipients such as churches or personal friends/contacts in ministry to address questions from believers/churches or certain situations that have arisen. The epistles sent to New Testament churches are: Romans, 1 and 2 Corinthians, Galatians, Ephesians, Philippians, Colossians, and 1 and 2 Thessalonians. Three epistles are designated as pastoral epistles and were sent from Paul to his friends: Timothy (1 and 2 Timothy) and Titus. The books that follow the pastoral epistles are deemed general epistles and include the books of Philemon, Hebrews, James, 1 and 2 Peter, 1, 2, and 3 John, and Jude. The seven letters contained in the book of Revelation also follow an epistolary format.

Since the above named twenty-one books are letters, they follow a format that was typical of correspondence written during the time of the New Testament. Often, the letter begins with a salutation from the author (though some are written anonymously, such as the book of Hebrews). The salutation is likely followed by a blessing or prayer for the recipients that then leads into the body of the letter. Sometimes the body of the letter may be divided into two general parts: doctrinal and ethical, which is often the case in Paul's letters. For example, the book of Ephesians may be divided in such a manner: chapters 1–3 lay the doctrinal foundation for chapters 4–6, which discuss the ethics of godly living. Bible students should be aware of this formula, since the imperative commands (what one must do) in the epistles are rooted in and accomplished solely by the indicative statements (what God has done).

Apocalyptic

The book of Revelation and portions of the book of Daniel are apocalyptic in nature. The word *apocalyptic* is an adjective that describes the events of the apocalypse, which Merriam-Webster describes as "one of the Jewish and Christian writings of 200 BC to AD 150 marked by . . . symbolic imagery, and the expectation of an imminent cosmic cataclysm in which God destroys the ruling powers of evil and raises the righteous to life in a messianic kingdom."[17] Yet, the term derives specifically from Rev 1:1, which begins, "The revelation of Jesus Christ. . . ." The word *revelation* in Greek is *apokalupsis* which means "uncovering" and speaks to the unveiling nature of apocalyptic literature. Thus, most of the apocalyptic material of the Bible comes from the last book of the Bible, Revelation, which was written by the apostle John around AD 65, making the book the final one to be written to close the biblical canon.

At the beginning, Revelation contains both its purpose and a promise of a blessing to come. In the first chapter and first verse of the book, John articulates the purpose of the revelation given to him by Jesus: "To show [Jesus's] servants what must soon take place" (Rev 1:1). Additionally, scholars note that Revelation is the only book that comes with a promise of blessing: "Blessed is the one who reads aloud the words of this prophecy, and blessed are those who hear the words of this prophecy and keep what is written in it, because the time is near" (Rev 1:3). These twin concepts of Revelation's stated purpose and the promise of blessing are founded upon John's assertion that the events will "soon take place" and the "time is near." John's word choice begs the question: To which time period do the events of Revelation describe and apply?

Four different categories describe how theologians seek to answer that question: *futurism*, *historicism*, *preterism*, and *idealism*, which are illustrated in the following table:

---

[17] *Merriam-Webster.com Dictionary*, s.v. "apocalypse," accessed August 5, 2021, https://www.merriam-webster.com/dictionary/apocalypse.

Interpretive Schools for the Book of Revelation	
Futurism	Believes the majority of events described in Revelation have not taken place yet and places great emphasis on interpreting the book as literally as possible. The futurist view is held by those who believe the Bible teaches a dispensational premillennialism and by those who believe in historical premillennialism. For those who read the book of Revelation from a dispensational premillennial viewpoint, large sections of the book after chapter 3 do not apply to the church today, since the events will take place during the Great Tribulation after the church has been raptured.
Historicism	Interprets events of the book as happening chronologically throughout world history. Sometimes held by historical premillennialists. Timothy Paul Jones notes, "Historical premillennialists try to balance symbolic and literal interpretations of Revelation, emphasizing both what the book meant to first-century readers and how it might apply to people's lives today."[18] This view is also consistent with postmillennialism or amillennialism.

---

[18] Timothy Paul Jones, *Four Views of the End Times: Views on Jesus' Second Coming* (Peabody, MA: Rose Publishing, 2006), loc. 117.

Idealism	Also called "iterism." Believes that the events described in the book of Revelation are a picture of the persecution of the church and its struggles throughout the church age (from Christ's ascension to his return again). This view divides Revelation into "seven sections. Instead of dealing with successive time-periods, these seven sections use apocalyptic language to describe the entire time from Jesus's first coming until his second coming in seven different ways."[19] This method is known as recapitulation (in contrast to a chronological presentation or interpretation). This view is typically held by amillennialists.
Preterism	Believes the majority of events described in the book of Revelation "occurred in the past, either in the period prior to the destruction of the Jerusalem temple in AD 70 or in the early Christian centuries leading up to the destruction of the Roman Empire in the fifth century AD."[20] This view is normally held by postmillennialists.

This chapter briefly discussed the various genres found within the Bible (narrative, law, poetry, wisdom, prophecy, gospels, epistles, and apocalyptic) to introduce the student to key components of each particular genre. Understanding the various types of literature contained in the Scriptures aids in proper biblical interpretation. Thus, to increase in biblical understanding, students should view learning about biblical genres as a lifelong pursuit, and therefore should make it a habit to read books of the Bible with the genre in mind, practice understanding texts in light of their

---

[19] Jones, loc. 155.

[20] Cornelis P. Venema, "Interpreting Revelation," January 1, 2012, https://www.ligonier.org/learn/articles/interpreting-revelation.

genre, and continue reading resources devoted to understanding the biblical genres.

For Further Study

A. Narrative: Readers may take a moment to read the book of Ruth and identify the three levels of the narrative (grasp the overall story of the book, consider the story's relationship to the progression of the story of God's people, Israel, and how the book of Ruth fits within the overarching narrative of the Bible). When considering the particular narrative of Ruth, students should identify the plot, the characters, and the setting.

B. Law: Readers may read Lev 25:1–22 and identify the category for the law (civil, ceremonial, moral) and anticipate the way(s) Christ is a fulfillment of the law. Readers may also read Exod 20:1–10 and consider the ways Christ fulfills these laws, how Christ reiterates each law in the New Testament, and the ways the three-fold use of the law provides insight in teaching the Ten Commandments.

4

Discovering the Meaning of the Text

Be diligent to present yourself to God as one
approved, a worker who doesn't need to be ashamed,
correctly teaching the word of truth.
—2 Timothy 2:15

In their book, *Effective Bible Teaching*, James C. Wilhoit and Leland Ryken discuss a common problem experienced by Bible teachers in the local church. They lament that Bible teachers often have "the inability to come to grips with a biblical text," describing the experience as one "where hard-working teachers . . . [can] never get a firm grip on a Bible passage. They . . . [stare] long and hard at the assigned passage, but seldom [do] all the pieces come together."[1] Thus, they note this problem is revealed in three ways:

1. The inability to teach a biblical passage in the terms of the kind of writing it is;
2. The prevailing failure to identify the big idea of a biblical passage;
3. The escape from the biblical text to other material.[2]

---

[1] James C. Wilhoit and Leland Ryken, *Effective Bible Teaching*, 2nd ed. (Grand Rapids: Baker Academic, 2012), 17.

[2] Wilhoit and Ryken, 17–19.

Consequently, they conclude that Bible teachers often drift into one of the five following types of Bible teaching:

1. "Paraphrasing" (recounting the passage without teaching its meaning)
2. "Allegorizing" (assigning an abstract, spiritual meaning to the passage)
3. "Moralizing" (making moral choices of biblical characters the main point of the passage)
4. "Spring-boarding" (ignoring the passage's meaning and discussing cross-references for the text)
5. Overusing "typology" (forcing the text to say something about Christ that is not discerned through the study of the text or how the text is interpreted by biblical authors).[3]

Each of these five types of Bible teaching have one element in common: they ignore the main idea of the text at hand, disregarding key principles of faithful, biblical interpretation. Some in the church may be unaware that a step-by-step process will aid them in understanding the Bible and teaching it to others. Evidently, Bible teachers must be equipped to teach the Scriptures in a way that is consistent with and not contrary to the pastoral task: "correctly teaching the Word of truth" (2 Tim 2:15). This chapter discusses the process of how to discover the meaning of a text by providing an introduction to and overview of the inductive method, along with its history and its relationship to other methods of interpretation employed throughout Christian history. Key terms such as *hermeneutics* are clearly defined.

Defining Hermeneutics

When people engage in the act of reading, they may or may not realize that they are inherently participating in a process whereby they seek to understand and comprehend the author's meaning. They consider the

---

[3] Wilhoit and Ryken, 18.

words (and definitions of those words) written by the author, the type of material they are reading, the intended audience, and the author's thesis, argument, or point. All these building blocks enable us to grasp what the author wrote, why they wrote it, and its significance. This process of reading comprehension is related to general hermeneutics, which is defined as "the methodological principles of interpretation."[4] Thus, biblical hermeneutics seeks to follow specific principles to discern the meaning of a text and is defined as a "discipline that studies the theory, principles, and methods used to interpret texts, especially ancient ones such as the sacred Scriptures."[5] It follows then that

> if the goal is correct understanding of communication, we need an approach and methods that are appropriate to the task. Hermeneutics provides the means for understanding the Scriptures and for applying that meaning responsibly. To avoid interpretation that is arbitrary, erroneous, or that simply suits personal whim, the reader needs methods and principles for guidance. A deliberate procedure to interpret based on sensible and agreed-upon principles becomes the best guarantee that an interpretation will be accurate. When we consciously set out to discover and employ such principles, we explore hermeneutics—biblical interpretation.[6]

Since biblical hermeneutics is a discipline, an art, or a science of interpretation, then Bible students must assess their own personal hermeneutic, which means that each person who comes to a biblical text has a "particular system of interpretation organized around an established frame of reference having an acknowledged set of presuppositions, values, or beliefs, which guides or controls the interpretation of texts."[7] To assess

---

[4] MacMillan Dictionary, s.v. "hermeneutics," accessed August 10, 2021, https://www.macmillandictionary.com/us/dictionary/american/hermeneutics.

[5] Hernando, *Dictionary of Hermeneutics* (see chap. 1, n. 21), 23.

[6] Klein, Blomberg, and Hubbard Jr., *Introduction to Biblical Interpretation* (see chap. 3, n. 7), 42.

[7] Hernando, *Dictionary of Hermeneutics*, 23.

one's personal hermeneutic, then, one must be cognizant of the fact that their initial reading of a text and study of it may be affected by previously held beliefs and preunderstandings. As Bauer and Traina note, "These presuppositions are thus necessarily present, but they are not necessarily correct; they may not actually coincide with the perspective of the text."[8] Thus, as students assess their personal hermeneutic, they must consider their preunderstandings of the text and the set of rules they employ or the method they most often use to determine the meaning of Scripture. One way to assess the adequacy of one's own personal method is to understand that many variables influence beliefs about interpretive steps, and one of those variables of influence is the history of interpretation in the church.

The History of Interpretation

To understand the development of hermeneutics, this section discusses the varying time periods of Christian history and how the church understood biblical interpretation at particular points in history. Each period (represented in the table below) in some sense impacts the modern evangelical reader when they engage in the process of discerning the meaning of a text.

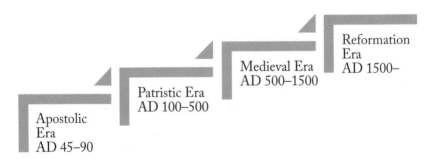

The graphic displays four foundational time periods that introduce Bible students to the early development of interpretive methods, specifically

---

[8] David R. Bauer and Robert A. Traina, *Inductive Bible Study: A Comprehensive Guide to the Practice of Hermeneutics* (Grand Rapids: Baker Academic, 2011), 35.

as they relate to interpretation in the evangelical world today. Each time period will be discussed briefly and broadly for a general understanding of the early history of interpretation.[9]

The Apostolic Era

During the time period of the early church, the presentation of biblical truth was through the preaching and (verbal) teaching of the apostles, as exemplified in the book of Acts. In addition to oral communication, the apostles and their acquaintances began to write about the life of Christ and the doctrines of the Christian faith (books and letters that would become part of the New Testament). Often, these writers interpreted Old Testament texts Christologically, determining passages that pointed to Jesus in shadows or types, explicitly quoting and/or explaining how those passages culminate in Christ in their writings for the early church. This mode of interpretation is called typology. Current Bible students may incorporate typology in their own study of the Old Testament, yet Plummer provides a helpful warning for the modern reader who reads the Old Testament typologically: "It seems safe to say that any typological use of the Old Testament not explicitly sanctioned in the New Testament should be entertained with great caution. Instead, we should focus on the literal meaning of the text."[10] Plummer's point at this juncture is helpful because, as Poythress notes, interpreters may fall into an extreme of inventing types according to the whim of the interpreter; yet Poythress identifies a second extreme—that of avoiding types altogether.[11] To avoid these two extremes, Poythress provides a helpful tool based

---

[9] For a more comprehensive understanding of the history of interpretation, see William W. Klein, Craig L. Blomberg, and Robert L. Hubbard Jr., "The History of Interpretation" in *Introduction to Biblical Interpretation*, 3rd ed. (Grand Rapids: Zondervan Academic, 2017), 66–116.

[10] Plummer, *40 Questions about Interpreting the Bible* (see chap. 3, n. 15), 86.

[11] Vern S. Poythress, "Edmund P. Clowney's Triangle of Typology in *Preaching and Biblical Theology*," *Unio cum Christo* 7, no. 2 (Oct 2021): 234–36.

upon Edmund Clowney's "Triangle of Typology." The basic elements for "doing typology well" proposed by Poythress include identifying:

1. The Old Testament symbol—"the tent"
2. The Anticipatory truth—"God dwells with his people"
3. The Fulfilled truth—"Christ dwells with his people in spiritual intensity and permanence."[12]

Thus, Poythress concludes,

> His [Clowney's] step 1 tells us to anchor our reasoning in what God revealed when he originally communicated a particular symbol. The tabernacle had a meaning for the Israelites. God explained it to them through Moses. . . . Clowney's step 2 . . . tells us to travel forward in the history of revelation. We need to see that the truth that God reveals at one point in history is not isolated but belongs to his comprehensive plan. . . . No symbolic meaning we find in the Old Testament stands in isolation. No meaning is just abandoned and dropped along the way to be permanently forgotten. All is moving toward the climax in Christ, which comes with not only his first coming but his second coming (2 Cor 1:20). The interpreter who avoids this richness of meaning out of fear of making a mistake is not doing justice to the unity and profundity and beauty of the plan of God, summed up in Christ (Eph 1:10).[13]

Another important element during the time of the early church was the collecting of the sacred writings or scrolls that would later lead to the formation of the Bible, wherein the books it should contain were identified, forming the canon. In their book, *Engaging Exposition*, the authors note that "as multiple works were written about Jesus, the church responded by discerning which writings were 'God-breathed' and then

---

[12] Poythress, 233.
[13] Poythress, 235–36.

collecting them for the benefit of the church."[14] This collection of books later came to be known as the New Testament canon.

The Patristic Era

The root word for *patristic* is *pater* which in Latin means "father," indicating that the patristic era concerns that period following the early church when "church fathers" began to engage with one another concerning core doctrines of the Christian faith. A key component of this time period is when "churches moved from simply recounting the oral stories about the ministry and teachings of Jesus to being able to read and study them. This reading and studying ushered in a whole new era of biblical proclamation. As a result, the early church soon recognized that pastor-teachers needed formal training to interpret the Scriptures."[15] The result of this need was the development of the Alexandrian school, and later the Antiochian school. While these schools historically have been presented as illustrating two differing viewpoints of biblical interpretation, "recent studies of the work of Antiochene and Alexandrian exegetes in the period have tended to conclude that it is hard to speak of differences in 'method' or even in hermeneutical principles between scholars in the two 'schools.'"[16] Therefore, this section emphasizes the interpretive principles derived from two patristic fathers (Irenaeus and Origen) rather than emphasizing one school over the other.

Irenaeus and the "Rule of Faith." The term *rule of faith* refers to "a summary of the apostolic testimony [that] served as a guidepost for understanding the redemptive story of the Bible and the profound work

---

[14] Akin, Curtis, and Rummage, *Engaging Exposition* (see chap. 1, n. 20), 15–16.

[15] Akin, Curtis, and Rummage, 18.

[16] Brian Daley, "Antioch and Alexandria: Christology as Reflection on God's Presence in History," *The Oxford Handbook on Christology*, September 2015, accessed January 11, 2022, https://www.oxfordhandbooks.com/view /10.1093/oxfordhb/9780199641901.001.0001/oxfordhb-9780199641901-e -43?print=pdf.

of salvation in Christ."[17] While the term refers to the "faith once for all delivered to the saints," that is, the creeds and doctrinal body of teaching that make up orthodox Christianity, early doctrinal development can be traced to Irenaeus and his writings on the Trinity. Stephen O. Presley notes that "in his short catechetical manual, *On Apostolic Preaching*, Irenaeus provides a summary of the rule of faith . . . [in which] Irenaeus assumes that the revelation given in the Scripture is inspired and therefore entirely consistent."[18] Presley goes on to explain that for Irenaeus,

> the Scriptures teach that there is only one God who is revealed as Father, Son, and Holy Spirit. As the rule unfolds, each person is characterized with scriptural language depicting their economic activity within the narrative structure of salvation history. Irenaeus assumes that when the Scriptures are read as a whole, they align with these three points of doctrine and this theological standard becomes the basic confession and tradition of the church derived from Scripture.[19]

Thus, the Bible as a whole teaches a body of doctrine, and that body of doctrine has been discerned, articulated, and defended over the course of church history. For example, the Nicene Creed serves as a summary of the rule of faith. In turn, the "rule of faith" applies to the practice of hermeneutics as it guides the interpretation of difficult texts. In other words, the exegete who derives theological truths from difficult texts does well to submit her interpretation to the "rule of faith" so that difficult texts are not misinterpreted.[20]

---

[17] Coleman M. Ford, "Salvation," in *Historical Theology for the Church*, ed. Jason G. Duesing and Nathan Finn (Nashville: B&H Academic, 2021), 91–92.

[18] Stephen O. Presley, "Scripture and Tradition," in *Historical Theology for the Church*, 82–83.

[19] Presley, 83.

[20] For an example of how the "rule of faith" serves as a guardrail for the interpretation of difficult texts, see R. Lucas Stamps, "The Trinity," in *Historical Theology for the Church*, 66.

One final contribution from Irenaeus to be noted concerns his promotion of a Christ-centered reading of the text that impacts the church today. Levy implies that Irenaeus

> . . . established an abiding exegetical principle: Scripture in its totality will be rendered coherent only when Christ the Word is understood to stand at the center of salvation history as it has been recorded across the Old and New Testaments. Both Testaments, in seamless continuity, relate the action of the divine Word throughout sacred time, culminating in the Word's incarnation. Old Testament prophecies are to be adduced as proof of history's fulfillment in the incarnate Word, who thereby confirms the unified work of the triune God, and the revelation of his will, across both Testaments.[21]

The Christ-centered emphasis from this early church father reminds interpreters that Jesus Christ is the subject of the entire story of God. Irenaeus, then, offers a legacy of both the rule of faith to guard against the misinterpretation of Scriptures and the importance of a Christ-centered understanding to guide Bible interpretation as a whole.

Origen and the "Three-fold Sense of Scripture." An approach to hermeneutics known as the "three-fold sense of Scripture" was first developed by Clement of Alexandria and later his student, Origen, who taught the idea that

> Scripture has three meanings:
>> (i) literal or physical;
>> (ii) moral or psychical; and
>> (iii) allegorical or intellectual

> The method employed, based upon the three meanings of Scripture, follows:
>> (i) every text has a deeper meaning which requires allegory;

---

[21] Ian Christopher Levy, *Introducing Medieval Biblical Interpretation: The Senses of Scripture in Premodern Exegesis* (Grand Rapids: Baker Academic, 2018), 8.

(ii) nothing unworthy of him should be said of God; and

(iii) nothing should be affirmed against the rule of faith . . . [which includes] the principles of the interpretation of Scripture by Scripture.[22]

Origen's method of interpretation will be further explored in the next section. As we will see, modern methods of interpretation are influenced not only by the patristics, but also by the methods developed during the medieval era as they expanded upon the work of the church fathers.

The Medieval Era

Building upon the three meanings of Scripture articulated by Clement and Origen, the medieval era depended heavily upon the allegorical method of interpretation. During this time, the three meanings of Scripture were expanded by John Cassian to the "fourfold use of Scripture" which insists that

Every biblical text has four levels of meaning:
1. literal;
2. moral;
3. spiritual (allegorical); and
4. heavenly (eschatological or anagogical).

Essentially, this fourth level of meaning was another allegorical level with heavenly or eschatological (end-times) nuances.[23]

Thus, Cassian "hand[ed] down what became the classic medieval paradigm of the four scriptural senses."[24] A traditional example of what the city of Jerusalem could mean in Old Testament texts according to the fourfold use of Scripture follows:

---

[22] Graeme Goldsworthy, *Gospel-Centered Hermeneutics: Foundations and Principles of Evangelical Biblical Interpretation* (Downers Grove, IL: IVP Academic, 2006), 95.

[23] Plummer, *40 Questions about Interpreting the Bible*, 90.

[24] Levy, *Introducing Medieval Biblical Interpretation*, 33.

Literal: "the city of God"
Allegorical: "the church"
Heavenly or Anagogical: "the heavenly city of God"
Moral or Tropological: "human soul that is either commended or castigated by God."[25]

The fourfold sense of biblical interpretation is the current method employed by the Catholic Church, described in the Catechism of the Catholic Church.[26] In evangelical circles, the four-fold use of Scripture can be associated with a negative connotation because of the emphasis evangelicals place upon authorial intent and interpreting texts in their "plain" sense or as they read literally. However, Matthew Emerson argues, in "In Defense of the Fourfold Method," that evangelicals should consider the fourfold use of Scripture for various reasons, mainly: 1) any allegorical uses of the Scripture for the patristics and medievalists in theory were supposed to be rooted in the literal meaning of the text; this means that the three spiritual senses (allegorical, anagogical, tropological) should not be isolated from the literal sense of the text. In other words, an allegorical interpretation must be tied to and rooted in the literal meaning of the text;[27] and 2) the fourfold use "helps us understand and interpret the Bible in a way that acknowledges its historical and literary detail without missing its bigger theological purpose,"[28] which Emerson then unpacks:

The allegorical sense demands that interpreters recognize the Bible's purpose of revealing Christ who reveals the Father; the tropological (or moral) sense demands that interpreters recognize the Bible's purpose of transforming believers into Christ's image; and the anagogical (or future sense) recognizes that a) the

---

[25] Levy, 33.

[26] Catechism of the Catholic Church, #115-119. Accessed August 11, 2021, https://www.vatican.va/archive/ENG0015/__PQ.HTM·

[27] Matthew Y. Emerson, "In Defense of the Fourfold Method," March 5, 2013, https://secundumscripturas.com/2013/03/05/in-defense-of-the-fourfold-method/.

[28] Emerson.

Bible is written as a metanarrative with a *telos* and b) that the tropological sense has a *telos* as well (to be completely like Christ; 1 John 3:2).[29]

Thus, consider how a Bible student committed to the literal sense might teach Psalm 122 and its verses concerning Jerusalem, both literally and allegorically. Psalm 122:6–7 says, "Pray for the well-being of Jerusalem: 'May those who love you be secure; may there be peace within your walls, security within your fortresses.'" The writer of the Psalm is David, and most Bible translations note that Psalm 122 is a song of ascents. These psalms were sung as the people of God processed up to the temple in the city of Jerusalem during the time of the feasts. Thus, verses 6–7 teach that God's people were to pray for a literal city that existed at a moment in time during the life of King David. Yet, as the New Testament unfolds, the church is alluded to as the New Jerusalem that will come down out of heaven at the end of the age (Rev 21:9–10). The literal sense should be considered, but the allegorical senses could fairly be put forth as applications of the text for the lives of readers today. Charles Spurgeon provides a great example of weaving the literal interpretation with an allegorical application as he relates these verses to the unity of the church in his sermon on Psalm 122. Concerning verse 7, Spurgeon proclaims, "Peace in the church should be our daily prayer, and in so praying we shall bring down peace upon ourselves."[30] His entire sermon on Psalm 122 is filled with examples of a Bible interpreter presenting the literal meaning and then offering an allegorical application. Consequently, many evangelicals likely use the fourfold sense of Scripture today that is rooted in interpretative methods of the medieval era; the commendation when incorporating the fourfold use, as Emerson notes above, is to root any allegory in the literal sense of the text.

---

[29] Emerson.

[30] Charles H. Spurgeon, "The Treasury of David: Psalm 122," The Spurgeon Archive, accessed August 16, 2021, https://archive.spurgeon.org/treasury/ps122.php.

Still, one emphasis of the medieval era must be considered before one can understand the Reformation period, which follows. The medieval era, as noted above, relied heavily upon allegorical interpretations of the Scriptures, and while the patristics intended that an allegorical use of Scripture be rooted in the literal sense, over time, the allegorical method was abused, often resulting in interpretations that were far removed from the authorial intent of a passage. An example of this comes from Bernard of Clairvaux and his allegorical interpretation of the Song of Songs. Additionally, the translation most often used was the Vulgate, which is the Latin translation of the Bible by Jerome, known to contain translation errors from the original Hebrew and Greek. The dependence upon the Vulgate, coupled with the abuse of the allegorical method, led to misinterpretations of the Bible. Furthermore, during this time period the Catholic Church upheld not only the Scriptures as authoritative, but also the authority of the church's traditions set forth by church councils and/or popes.[31] Consequently, two precursors to the Reformation should be noted. First, during the late Middle Ages, John Wycliffe pointed to a new trend that would eventually come to bear in the Reformation. Gerald Bray contends that "for Wycliffe, Scripture contained all truth, and human knowledge was useless by comparison. Nothing which could not be found in Scripture had any place in true religion" and "the fathers of the church he regarded as useless, unless what they said corresponded to what the Scriptures plainly taught."[32] Second, a new Latin translation of the Greek New Testament by Erasmus in 1516 "exposed many translation errors in the Latin Vulgate and undermined the absolute authority it had enjoyed in supporting church doctrine" ultimately "cast[ing] shadows of doubt on the authority of the [Roman Catholic Church].[33]

---

[31] Klein, Blomberg, and Hubbard Jr., *Introduction to Biblical Interpretation*, 86–92.

[32] Gerald Bray, *Biblical Interpretation: Past and Present* (Downers Grove, IL: InterVarsity, 1996), 154.

[33] Klein, Blomberg, and Hubbard Jr., *Introduction to Biblical Interpretation*, 92.

The Reformation Era

The first chapter, entitled "The Nature of the Bible," considered seven core characteristics of the Scripture: *inspiration, inerrancy, infallibility, authority, necessity, sufficiency,* and *clarity*. These attributes of Scripture find echoes in the apostolic era, the patristic era, and the medieval era but are further developed in church history during the time of the Reformation. The preceding section on the medieval era set the stage for the events of the Reformation as God began to revive in his people a desire to study the written Word, understand it, and live accordingly.

One such person who was revived by studying the Bible was Martin Luther, a Catholic monk who was incredibly burdened by the weight of his sin. While studying the book of Romans, Luther was born again when he came to understand that "the righteous shall live by faith" (Rom 1:17). Though Luther came to understand that salvation is by grace through faith in his study of Romans, he had already experienced disillusionment with some of the teachings of the Roman Catholic Church before his conversion. The church practiced the selling of "indulgences" (which were papal promises to remove the penalty of purgatory to those who bought them) to facilitate the rebuilding of St. Peter's Basilica in Rome. Luther articulated his belief in the unbiblical nature of the practice of indulgences in his *95 Theses* that he famously nailed to the door at the church in Wittenberg, Germany. Eventually, his pamphlet would become highly circulated, and while he had initially intended to enter a conversation with the church on indulgences, he and the church would come to an impasse that resulted in Luther's excommunication from the Catholic Church and lit a flame for what is known today as the Protestant Reformation.

The story of Martin Luther and its implications regarding evangelical interpretive methods cannot be underestimated, for "at the heart of this important story lie questions of authority and—intrinsically connected to these—biblical interpretation."[34] For the first time, Luther was exhib-

---

[34] Iain Provan, *The Reformation and the Right Reading of Scripture* (Waco, TX: Baylor University Press, 2017), 6.

iting very publicly "an appeal to Scripture by an individual over against the Church [which was] not to be tolerated."[35] Thus, Provan highlights several impactful features resulting in the Reformation principle of *sola Scriptura* (literally "Scripture alone"—the belief that Scripture alone is the authority for the believer's faith and practice):

1. A determination of which books should be included in the canon—ultimately solidifying the Protestant position that the books of the Apocrypha should remain outside the canon
2. A commitment to studying the Bible in the original languages (Hebrew, Greek, and Aramaic)
3. A belief that the Scriptures are clear and able to be understood by anyone who could read
4. A strong opposition to an allegorical reading of Scripture and a defense of discerning the "literal sense" of a text
5. An interpretive method dependent upon the concept of the "analogy of Scripture" wherein "nothing should be inferred from a difficult or unclear passage that is not evident from other, clearer passages" (sometimes called the "analogy of faith")
6. A reliance upon the Holy Spirit to awaken the reader to understand God's inspired, infallible Word[36]

And while the Reformation opposed allegorical readings of the Bible, Bray notes that "combating allegorical interpretations of the Old Testament, without losing its Christological significance, was a major preoccupation of the Reformers."[37] Thus, to continue in the tradition of the Protestant Reformation, for those completely opposed to allegory, the Reformers' fight for a Christ-centered interpretation is instructive. Yet, an introduction to the Reformation era is not complete without mentioning John Calvin and his impact upon exegesis. First, one must understand that Calvin's system of theology, Covenantalism, significantly impacted the way he read and taught Scripture. Calvin believed that the overarching

---

[35] Provan, 7.
[36] Provan, 8–12.
[37] Bray, *Biblical Interpretation: Past and Present*, 172.

story of the Bible is told through covenants, which illustrates his belief in the unity of the Bible between the Old and New Testaments. Second, Calvin wrote commentaries and sermons that are studied and referenced today in modern exegesis. These works illustrated Calvin's commitment "to unfold the text of the Bible so that the listener could understand it as easily as possible. Therefore, he sought to preach strictly upon the literal text of the Bible, to interpret it accurately and simply, and to apply it to the lives of the listeners. His methodology in doing so can be summarized into three main principles":

1. Conciseness and simplicity (for the common person)
2. Verse-by-verse exegesis
3. *Lectio continua* (sequentially through an entire book).[38]

Current Methods of Interpretation

The history of interpretation informs the methods of interpretation this book seeks to discuss, and while the area of biblical hermeneutics continued to expand after the Reformation, the main foundation for evangelical hermeneutics is based upon the approaches developed during the eras of the patristics, the medieval church, and the Reformation. A technique that finds its roots, then, in all three eras, is known as the historical-grammatical method, which was developed by a Lutheran theologian named Johann August Ernesti. The goal of the historical-grammatical method is to discover the meaning of biblical texts within their context, seeking to discern the idea the original author intended for the original audience. The inductive Bible study method, which reflects the historical-grammatical system, is a popular step-by-step process that enables readers to discover the meaning of a text and has been widely used since the 1950s.

In 1952, Robert A. Traina first published his book *Methodological Bible Study: A New Approach to Hermeneutics*, which outlined a process for studying the Bible according to the following steps: observation,

---

[38] David Eung Yul Ryoo, "Learning from Calvin's Methodology of Biblical Interpretation," *Unio cum Christo* 3, no. 2 (Oct 2017): 27–28.

interpretation, evaluation, application, and correlation.[39] A well-known Bible teacher named Kay Arthur also popularized the inductive method with her book *How to Study Your Bible*, which was originally published in 1976, using the steps of observation, interpretation, and application. Other authors have made unique contributions to the inductive Bible study method. In 1998, Lawrence O. Richards and Gary J. Bredfeldt published their book, *Creative Bible Teaching*, pointing the reader to following five steps: observation, interpretation, generalization, application, and implementation. In 2014, Jen Wilkin influenced Bible study methods with her book, *Women of the Word: How to Study the Bible with Both Our Hearts and Our Minds*, suggesting the three steps of comprehension, interpretation, and application. In 2016, Richard Alan Fuhr Jr. and Andreas J. Köstenberger wrote *Inductive Bible Study: Observation, Interpretation, and Application through the Lenses of History, Literature, and Theology*. They retained the three steps of observation, interpretation, and application, as seen in Kay Arthur's books on the subject, but incorporated the "hermeneutical triad" of history, genre, and theology.

This text uses the inductive Bible study steps introduced by Richards and Bredfeldt in *Creative Bible Teaching*: observation, interpretation, generalization, application, and implementation. The following chapters introduce the reader to each of the five steps to help Bible students easily engage in the process of hermeneutics whereby they employ the historical-grammatical method of discerning the meaning of the text the original biblical author intended for the original recipients. As students understand the process behind each step, this will aid in preventing the problems noted by Wilhoit and Ryken at the beginning of this chapter. The inductive Bible study process enables students to teach Bible passages according to their literary genre, equips students to identify the main idea of a passage, and prevents the desire to look to extra-biblical material because the student is thoroughly prepared to engage the Bible.

---

[39] For a more detailed understanding of the history of the Inductive Bible Study Method, see David R. Bauer and Robert A. Traina, *Inductive Bible Study: A Comprehensive Guide to the Practice of Hermeneutics* (Grand Rapids: Baker Academic, 2011), 1–2.

5

Observing the Text

Never take the word of truth from my mouth, for I hope
in your judgments. I will always obey your instruction,
forever and ever. I will walk freely in an open place because
I study your precepts. I will speak of your decrees before
kings and not be ashamed. I delight in your commands,
which I love. I will lift up my hands to your commands,
which I love, and will meditate on your statutes.
—Psalm 119:43–48

The verses from Psalm 119 quoted above illustrate a prayer of joy from someone who has steeped in God's Word. For those who make a practice of studying the Bible, a feeling of comradery with the psalmist cannot be helped—he prays that God's Word would never be removed from his mouth, because in it he finds hope. He comments that he will obey God's instruction eternally and that he has gained a sense of freedom through the principles found in the Scriptures. He does not fear embarrassment or shame at speaking the Word before those who have rule and authority over his life. He declares his delight in and his love for God's commands. He positions himself in a posture that both receives and plans for continued mental energy to be spent on contemplating the Bible. The psalmist deeply loves God and his Word. And so it is (or should be) with every person who has been redeemed by Christ. For those who resonate with the words of the psalmist, they know that there is both a richness and a depth to God's Word. The more one reads and studies it, the more it fills and satisfies the heart while at the same time it causes a thirst for more.

This book seeks to put tools into the hands of those who crave God's Word. While the details below may seem intricate at times, never forget that the entire point is to enjoy God's Word, that ultimately joy and delight may be found in the triune God of the universe. For nothing else in the world can bring as much joy as when Christ and his Word are considered, as the apostle Peter so aptly confessed: "Lord, to whom will we go? You have the words of eternal life" (John 6:68).

The last chapter noted that biblical hermeneutics seeks to follow specific principles to discern the meaning of a text and was defined as a "discipline that studies the theory, principles, and methods used to interpret texts, especially ancient ones such as the sacred Scriptures."[1] The specific discipline to interpret biblical texts is based upon the historical-grammatical method, which finds its foundation in Christian history from the time of the apostles through the Reformation period. The inductive Bible study process, developed in the latter half of the twentieth century, provides clear and accessible steps to discern the meaning of a text and apply it to the life of the Christian. Thus, inductive Bible study is the process whereby readers are invited to exegete a passage (from the word *exegesis*, which means "drawing out the meaning of a biblical text").

Those who do not know how to exegete a text may fall into a practice of reading meaning into the text, otherwise known as *eisegesis*. When one "eisegetes" a text, they insert meaning into the passage that the author of the text did not intend. The example of medieval interpreters who abused the allegorical method illustrates a form of eisegeis, but many Christian preachers and Bible teachers today are guilty of the same type

---

[1] Hernando, *Dictionary of Hermeneutics* (see chap. 1, n. 21), 23.

of misreading and misinterpretation of Scripture. Richards and Bredfeldt hint at this way of teaching:

> Curriculum producers and Bible teachers often use the Bible to teach to their own developmental and behavioral objectives rather than actually teaching what the Bible teaches. [The concern is that] the Bible is merely being used as a jumping-off point for teaching. Much of Bible teaching simply uses the Bible to teach ideas that are only loosely related to the teaching of Scripture.[2]

To be sure, both men and women have engaged in this sort of "Bible" teaching. From small group teachers to big name conference speakers and everywhere in between—teaching that is devoid of the true point of the passage is a concern, because as Richards and Bredfeldt go on to imply, "ideas loosely related" to the Bible have no power to transform the individual listener. Rather, change takes place in the lives of Christians when God's Spirit moves within them through the power of his Word. Of course, the ministry of the Word takes place as Christians attend church weekly and sit under the regular preaching of the Bible done by their pastor/elders, as well as through the spiritual discipline of personal Bible study. Yet, women who have the opportunity to disciple other women and who have been given the spiritual gift of teaching for the edification of the body need to be equipped to teach the Word, which is the theme and purpose of this book. Therefore, a call to teach the Scriptures by exegeting each and every text begins with understanding the inductive process and its first step of observation.

The Inductive Method

To better comprehend the inductive process, the word *inductive* should be considered. An illustration from the well-known character Sherlock Holmes brings clarity on inductive reasoning versus deductive reasoning, as it applies to the interpretation of biblical texts. Sir Arthur Conan

---

[2] Richards and Bredfeldt, *Creative Bible Teaching* (see chap. 1, n. 9), 66.

Doyle's character, Sherlock, is famous for using inductive reasoning to solve mysterious murder cases. Readers surely are familiar with the method he employs—he gathers clues and uses critical thinking to form his answers on the who, what, why, where, when, and how of a case. Holmes does not begin with a foregone conclusion but rather uses hints along the way to lead him to the culprit of the crimes he investigates. The system employed by Sherlock, then, is known as inductive reasoning. Bauer and Traina explain the concept as it applies to Bible study:

> We should begin by indicating what we mean by *induction*. The term *inductive* . . . in the broader sense involves a commitment to move from the evidence of the text and the realities that surround the text to possible conclusions (or inferences) regarding the meaning of the text. In this sense, *inductive* is practically synonymous with *evidential* over against *deductive*, which is presuppositional, involving a movement from presuppositions with which one approaches the text to a reading of the text intended to support these presuppositions.[3]

The emphasis on inductive reasoning rather than on deductive methods for Bible study does not necessarily mean that deductive reasoning is wrong or unhelpful, "but for those who seek to discover what the Bible means, an assumption-oriented approach to the meaning of individual texts is counterproductive and impedes discovery."[4] Thus, while Bible students come to different Scriptures with preconceived notions of what a text means, it is best to let inductive study of the text inform the student's understanding of the text; this mode of interpretation is the foundation of expository teaching. This means that a student may come to the text with a preunderstanding of the meaning of the text (which is distinct from coming to the text with a set of presuppositions—such as believing that the Bible is inerrant, infallible, sufficient, and unified). For example,

---

[3] Bauer and Traina, *Inductive Bible Study* (see chap. 4, n. 8), 1.

[4] Richard Alan Fuhr Jr. and Andreas J. Köstenberger, *Inductive Bible Study: Observation, Interpretation, and Application through the Lenses of History, Literature, and Theology* (Nashville: B&H Academic, 2016), 35.

when one relies upon topical teaching, they may use deductive methods by coming to a text with a general idea that they wish to communicate, which they then go to the Bible to find a Scripture that supports the general idea they would like to teach. If the teacher is biblically literate, they may end up teaching the true exegetical idea of the text that supports the idea they wish to teach. However, if a teacher is not careful, this method may very well lead to what is known as proof-texting (which is defined as taking Scripture out of its original context and using it to prove a thought or idea that may or may not be related to the biblical author's meaning and purpose).

A classic example of proof-texting comes from using Phil 4:13 to teach the idea that Christ can empower people to do what they desire. The well-known verse states, "I am able to do all things through him who strengthens me." Many have noted that the verse has been plastered on coffee cups, journals, T-shirts, as well as on athletes as they compete in football, etc. The question, however, is did the apostle Paul, when he wrote to the church at Philippi, intend for the members of that church to apply the verse to whatever they wanted to accomplish in life? Did he truly mean to convey that Christ's power is available to the athlete who desires to win? Or to the student who wishes to make a good grade? Deductive reasoning might take the verse at face value and apply it exactly that way. But a teacher who has observed the passage will discern that Phil 4:13 is not a catchall verse for all of life. Rather, the verse's meaning must be discerned through reading the immediate context (the surrounding verses) and the remote context (the entire book of Philippians). For reference, consider Phil 4:10–14 in its entirety:

> I rejoiced in the Lord greatly because once again you renewed your care for me. You were, in fact, concerned about me but lacked the opportunity to show it. I don't say this out of need, for I have learned to be content in whatever circumstances I find myself. I know how to make do with little, and I know how to make do with a lot. In any and all circumstances I have learned the secret of being content—whether well fed or hungry, whether in abundance or in need. I am able to do all things through him

who strengthens me. Still, you did well by partnering with me in my hardship.

The immediate context shows that in verses 11–12, Paul says, ". . . for I have learned to be content in whatever circumstances I find myself. I know how to make do with little, and I know how to make do with a lot. In any and all circumstances I have learned the secret of being content—whether well fed or hungry, whether in abundance or in need." Then, Paul immediately tells the reader in the following verse the secret for finding true contentment, which is that he is able to do all things through Christ who gives him strength. Thus, the "all" that Paul can do through Christ is qualified and relates to his progression of thought in the immediate context (vv. 11–12). Mainly that in the midst of need or want, Paul is able to be content because he is in union with Christ. It is Christ who strengthens him to "do all things"—the "all things" that he can do is the ability to be content, no matter the life circumstance he finds himself in. His source of joy is not present circumstances; his source of joy is Jesus. Paul can be hungry or full, because he has Christ. Paul can live in abundance or need, because he has Christ. This thought is tied to the overall theme of Philippians because despite Paul's circumstance of being imprisoned (Phil 1:7, 12–14), Paul has boldly stated that for him, to live is Christ and to die is gain (Phil 1:21), and therefore he has learned that Christ Jesus himself is contentment.

    The truth of Phil 4:13—that Jesus is the true source of contentment—brings great delight to the soul and abundant glory to Christ beyond a "man-centered" misapplication of the verse, where Christ is a means to an end rather than being the glorious end himself. Thus, the true meaning of the verse is eloquently stated by a Puritan writer of long ago in his book, *The Rare Jewel of Christian Contentment*: "Therefore [Paul's] meaning must be, 'I find a sufficiency of satisfaction in my own heart, through the grace of Christ that is in me. Though I have not outward comforts and worldly conveniences to supply my necessities, yet I have a sufficient portion between Christ and my soul abundantly to satisfy me in every condition.'"[5]

---

[5] Jeremiah Burroughs, *The Rare Jewel of Christian Contentment* (Carlisle, PA: The Banner of Truth Trust, 2013), 18.

Thus, one may conclude that "induction [rather than deductive reasoning] . . . is more suitable to the study of the Bible because you compile the evidence and then, proceeding from your analysis of the evidence, reach probable, albeit at times tentative, conclusions."[6] The pursuit of evidence to form a conclusion based upon analysis of that evidence is reminiscent of the process historians embark upon in historical research. As a history minor at the undergraduate level, I was given an assignment once that came to me in the form of a packet containing pictures, letters, and newspaper clippings about a couple who lived in the early 1900s in the town where my college was located. Students were instructed to examine the contents of the packet to determine and write out what we perceived was the couple's life narrative. This assignment forced students to consider their own practice of historical method—would they spend the necessary time poring over the packet's contents in order to re-create a timeline and narrative, or would they make up a narrative loosely based upon the packet's materials? One choice reflects proper historical method while the other reveals a careless, indifferent attitude. The same choices are presented to Bible students when they are given the task of interpretation. They must take the time to observe the text and gather details to understand the true meaning. And yet, four elements cause distance between the Bible student and the biblical text:

Distance of Culture

The Old and New Testaments were written with several different cultures at play in the background. Scholars often note that the culture was highly agrarian, meaning the lifestyle of most characters in the Bible related to owning and cultivating land. The culture of today reflects the advances of modern technology, yet the Bible often reflects a primitive life unfamiliar to the contemporary reader. Additionally, the Pentateuch (the first five books of the Bible, called the Law) instituted rituals and practices that constituted religious and civic life for the nation of Israel, which formed

---

[6] Fuhr Jr. and Köstenberger, *Inductive Bible Study*, 35.

Hebrew culture distinct from the practices of society in the twenty-first century. The same is true of the New Testament, which contains not only the Jewish culture of the Old Testament but also the cultures related to ancient Rome and Greece. The challenge for the average Bible student is continued growth in understanding the cultures that form the backdrop of both Old and New Testament texts.

Distance of Geography

Many Bibles contain maps of the various locations seen in the Old and New Testaments. The maps give Bible students a rough picture of the landscape and countries during different time periods in biblical history; for example, the path of the exodus from Egypt to the Promised Land, the allotment of land to the twelve tribes, Israel during the life and reign of King David, Israel during the life and ministry of Jesus, and the missionary journey paths of the apostle Paul. These maps illustrate the distance of geography from the present world along with current countries and their borders, representing how far removed the modern reader is from ancient times. Thus, students must recognize the lack of connection they have with the places mentioned in biblical narratives and the epistles so they can obtain a more informed understanding and interpretation of texts.

Distance of Language

The original manuscripts of the Bible are written in Hebrew, Koine Greek (also known as Hellenistic Greek), and Aramaic. Most Bible students do not know any of these three languages and may never have the opportunity to study them in a comprehensive manner that would render the ability to read and translate Bible texts, or even discern the idioms unique to each language. Thus, anyone who reads the Scriptures in English must be aware of their own particular dependence upon another's ability and faithfulness in translation, as well as the original manuscript used by the translator and the translator's philosophy. For example, the *New American Standard Bible* (NASB), published by the Lockman Foundation, relies upon the Hebrew manuscripts, *Biblia Hebraica* and the Dead Sea Scrolls, and for the Greek, it uses *Novum Testamentum Graece*. The NASB is translated word-for-word (also known as "formal equivalence"), meaning the translators operate from the philosophy that the Scriptures should be rendered as literally as possible from the original text for the modern reader. In contrast, the *New International Version* (NIV) is translated thought-for-thought (also known as "dynamic equivalence"), meaning the translation philosophy considers the original text and how the translator can reveal the thought or meaning of the passage in modern language in a way that a contemporary reader would understand. Additionally, the NIV uses the same manuscripts as the NASB. However, Bibles such as the *King James Version* and the *New King James Version* rely upon different manuscripts for the translation process resulting in varying degrees of differences from other translations like the NASB, ESV, and NIV.

Thus, the Bible student is largely reliant upon translators and translation philosophies unique to the particular translation they choose, underscoring the language distance that may directly impact interpretation. For instance, the Greek word transliterated as *gune* can either mean "woman" or "wife." Translators depend upon context when confronted with the choice of translating *gune* as either woman or wife, but sometimes the choice of how the word should be translated is unclear. In 1 Timothy 3, in the section on deacons, the NASB renders the word as "women" while the ESV translates the word as "wives." The interpretation of the text depends upon the translation of the word, for the ESV promotes the understanding that the apostle Paul is providing characteristics that a male deacon's wife should display, while the NASB could be seen as promoting the view that women, not just men, may serve as deacons. Most people who read either the NASB or the ESV are unaware of these small nuances due to the distance of language.

Distance of Time

As noted under "distance of culture," the times of the Bible are far removed from modernity. Readers can study the historical time periods reflected in the Scriptures and yet the great distance of time from

Genesis 1 to current day decreases understanding. Bible students should recognize that knowing other eras is based on informed study and is dependent largely on what other have studied and taught; therefore, we should research the time period related to our particular text and then re-create the biblical world using our imagination, building on available scholarship. We engage this task to lessen the distance of time.

Consequently, the Bible must be studied because we are separated from the world of the Scriptures by culture, geography, language, and time. Other scholars have concluded:

> We need a systematic approach to interpreting Scripture because the Bible was originally written
> - to somebody else
> - who lived a long time ago
> - in another part of the world
> - where they spoke a different language
> - and had different cultural values.[7]

The "systematic approach" of inductive Bible study will aid modern Bible students as they seek to interpret biblical passages. The first step to that process is "observation."

The Purpose and Process of Observing a Text

Inductive Bible study begins with step one: observation, which is a process that seeks to answer the question, "What does the text say?" As students seek to draw out the meaning of the text, the initial action of observation involves "roaming" through a passage. The acronym, "ROAM," is a colloquial method taught in various inductive Bible study texts and groups.[8] Bible students can easily observe all elements of a passage by remembering that they should ROAM:

---

[7] Klein, Blomberg, and Hubbard Jr., *Introduction to Biblical Interpretation* (see chap. 3, n. 7), 59.

[8] I was introduced to "ROAM" in a seminary course titled "Principles of Teaching," taught by Dr. Bradley C. Thompson.

- **R** = Read (the text)
- **O** = (write down) Observations
- **A** = Ask (questions)
- **M** = Meditate (on the text)

While these steps below are listed sequentially, the process of roaming through a passage does not have to necessarily follow a step-by-step pattern. Some may find that the process is more interactive, with reading leading to observing to asking questions, which may send them back to reading, which in turn may lead to meditation. Each step is described below but should be incorporated in a manner that fits the style and personality of the student.

Read

Reading a Bible passage that is being studied is an action that may seem obvious. Yet, the type of reading being done is not superficial or hurried. When someone reads the Bible to glean its meaning, they cannot and should not read quickly and cursorily. Reading should be exercised deliberately, slowly, joyfully, and critically.

Deliberate reading is thoughtful. It considers every word, every sentence, and every paragraph. It seeks to understand the meaning of the words and how the sentences are crafted, along with the writer's flow of logic displayed throughout paragraphs. Thus, deliberate reading is slow and is able to tune out distractions of news, social media, relationships, and daily tasks that might weigh upon us. Reading a passage slowly leads to reading the Bible joyfully and awakens the thought processes and one's "sanctified imagination" to delight in Christ and his Word.[9] It seeks to comprehend and grasp at God himself through the pages of the Bible, working to know God and his person. John Piper eloquently describes the joy of reading the Bible in his book *Reading the Bible Supernaturally*, pointing out that "the Scriptures are written to create in us a savoring of

---

[9] The term *sanctified imagination* is used by preachers and authors, and likely can be traced back to A. W. Tozer.

the glories of Christ. How then can we ever come to the Scriptures as if the only aim were practical guidelines or doctrinal clarification? No. . . . We will go to see and savor the glories of all that God is for us in Jesus."[10]

Every time a Bible student sits down to study and observe the Scriptures, she must read with the ultimate goal of beholding Christ in his Word, having her soul satisfied by God's Word as daily bread and by Christ himself, the bread of life. So, the Bible student reads deliberately, slowly, joyfully, and finally critically. The use of the word *critical* means that the student should engage with God's Word using critical thinking to determine how one passage relates to another. Reading the Bible should be a skill that continues to develop throughout the life of the student, so that as one text is read, another text comes to mind, helping us to connect one passage to the whole of the Bible.

To read the Bible deliberately, slowly, joyfully, and critically, several methods are suggested. First, the specific passage being studied should be read multiple times. Various professors will give a number at this point, but the overall emphasis is to read the passage over, and over, and over again. Multiple readings of the particular passage must also be tied to multiple readings of the entire book of the Bible from which the passage is derived. For instance, if one were studying Heb 4:14–16, the student should not just read that particular text numerous times but also the entire book of Hebrews multiple times. This allows us to understand the passage in relation to the whole book of Hebrews and to determine if we have chosen the correct starting place (v. 14) and the correct ending place (v. 16) (essentially known as "determining the limits of a passage") without cutting out or missing a logical piece to an argument in an epistle or a major piece of the story in a narrative. A hint to help determine the limits of a passage would be to notice if the text stands alone in one paragraph. Hebrews 4:14–16 contains three verses that are set off into one paragraph (see the CSB, ESV, NASB, and NIV). This means the translators for each version believed that the author of Hebrews was shifting to a new

---

[10] John Piper, *Reading the Bible Supernaturally: Seeing and Savoring the Glory of God in Scripture* (Wheaton, IL: Crossway, 2017), 125.

point or flow of logic in his argument. The student, however, should not solely depend upon translators, thoughts but should consider if a preceding or following verse should be included in the study of the text to make sure the Bible author's point is being fully considered in context.

Additionally, the student should read the passage in the original language if the student has the ability to do so, and should translate the passage from the original language, if possible. If the student does not have translating abilities, she should consider reading the passage in four different translations (at least). It is recommended that the four translations be from the NASB (word-for-word), the ESV (word-for-word), the Christian Standard Bible (CSB, which employs "optimal equivalence" as a translation philosophy over and against formal equivalence or dynamic equivalence), and the NIV (thought-for-thought).[11]

Reading the passage in multiple translations aids in identifying "textual variations" when one English word has been chosen over another English word in the translation process (as in the case of the Greek word, *gune*, which means "wife" or "woman," discussed previously). If different words appear in a verse in the passage being studied from one English translation to the next, the student should mark the textual variations as "exegetical difficulties" to consider during the interpretive process if the difference in word choice potentially changes the meaning of the passage. This specific action step is important because "whenever translations have truly significant differences between them, there is a sure indication that some exegetical difficulty lies behind the differences."[12]

---

[11] The introduction to the CSB states, "The CSB uses optimal equivalence as its translation philosophy. In the many places throughout the Bible where a word-for-word rendering is understandable, a literal translation is used. When a word-for-word rendering might obscure the meaning for a modern audience, a more dynamic translation is used." *The Holy Bible: Christian Standard Version* (Nashville: Holman Bible Publishers, 2017), viii.

[12] Gordon D. Fee, *New Testament Exegesis: A Handbook for Students and Pastors*, rev. ed. (Louisville: Westminster/John Knox Press, 1993), 37–38.

Observe

As students read the Bible passage multiple times in various translations, several observations should begin to stand out. An observation is defined as information gleaned through the act of noticing or perceiving. The simple act of writing out each observation for a text leads to the following steps of asking questions and meditating upon the contents of the passage, which in turn may lead to more questions and thoughtful meditation. Students should state the obvious items seen from the passage as a whole as well as insights gleaned from individual verses, individual sentences, distinct phrases, and singular words. The process of observation should be viewed as an enjoyable practice that leads one down a path of discovery into the treasury of God's Word. For example, consider Heb 4:14–16 again, which says,

> Therefore, since we have a great high priest who has passed through the heavens—Jesus the Son of God—let us hold fast to our confession. For we do not have a high priest who is unable to sympathize with our weaknesses, but one who has been tempted in every way as we are, yet without sin. Therefore, let us approach the throne of grace with boldness, so that we may receive mercy and find grace to help us in time of need.

Students should list out as many observations per verse and for the entire text as possible. For example, here are five observations for verse 14 alone:

1. The passage begins with the word "therefore," indicating that the following verses are built upon a point made earlier by the author.
2. "Let us hold fast to our confession" is one of two commands in the passage.
3. The command "let us hold fast to our confession" is predicated upon the fact that "we have a great high priest who has passed through the heavens."
4. The great high priest is none other than Jesus the Son of God.
5. The author is speaking to a group of people, not an individual person, using words like "we" and "us."

If one were to list observations for the entire passage itself, she might note repeated words throughout the text, which points out the writer's main idea. In Heb 4:14–16, the words "we" and "us" are repeated, as well as "high priest." Another observation about the entire passage would be that there are two commands (also known as imperatives): to hold fast to a confession and to approach the throne of grace boldly. These commands are based upon the indicative statements, forming the foundation for holding fast and approaching boldly, mainly that the believer is able to obey these two commands because Jesus the Son of God, the great high priest, has passed through the heavens and has been tempted as we are, yet without sin.

Ask Questions

As students work through reading and making observations of the text, they will naturally begin to form questions. Consider Heb 4:14–16 again. While the student may have listed many observations for each verse and the text as a whole, they should also ask questions about those observations. Asking who, what, where, when, and how is a great pattern to follow, for example:

1. What is the word "therefore" there for?
2. Who is the word "we" in verses 14, 15, and 16 referring to?
3. How has the term "great high priest" been used by the author of Hebrews before this point?
4. What does the term "great high priest" mean?
5. Where else (or) has the term "great high priest" been used in the New Testament?
6. Where else (or) has the term "great high priest" been used in the Old Testament?
7. What does it mean that our great high priest has "passed through the heavens?"
8. Why does the writer specifically refer to Jesus as the "Son of God" at this particular point? Why not "Son of Man" or another title of Christ?

9.   What is the "confession" that we are to "hold fast to"?

10. What does it mean to "hold fast"?

The first three steps of ROAM (reading, observing, and asking questions) lead to meditation.

Meditate

As students work through reading a passage, observing it and asking questions, they will be involved in meditating on the passage. This act is to simply think deeply and prayerfully over both the observations made and the questions asked. Meditation upon a Bible passage should be undertaken by the help of the Holy Spirit, knowing that the Spirit is at work in every person who is in Christ, revealing truth to them. Jesus teaches about the work of the Holy Spirit in John 15:26–16:15 and tells the disciples that the Spirit proceeds from the Father and testifies about Christ (15:26), that Jesus himself will send the Counselor to them (16:7), that the work of the Spirit is to convict the world of sin, righteousness, and judgment (16:8), that the Spirit is the Spirit of truth and will guide them into truth, declare what is to come, will glorify Christ, and will declare what belongs to Christ to them (16:12–15). Thus, the work of the Spirit as laid out for the disciples in John 15–16 has great implications for the believer who is meditating upon God's Word, because

> he guides into all the truth, that is into the whole body of redemptive revelation. . . . He never stresses one point of doctrine at the expense of all the others. He leads into all the truth. Moreover, in the carrying out of this task he stands in intimate relationship to the other persons of the Trinity. We read: "for he will not speak of himself, but whatever he hears he will speak." Father and Spirit are one in essence. What the Spirit hears from the Father he, in and through the Word, whispers into the hearts of believers. He is ever searching the depths of God. He comprehends them and reveals them to God's children (1 Cor 2:10, 11).[13]

---

[13] William Hendriksen, *New Testament Commentary: Exposition of the Gospel According to John* (Grand Rapids: Baker Book House, 2004), 328.

The work of the Holy Spirit, then, should encourage the Bible student who engages in meditating upon the text. The word *meditate* in Hebrew literally means "to mutter or to muse." Thus, one can mutter the text to oneself, thinking through the words and phrases, and the meaning that is being conveyed. This should be done prayerfully, seeking the aid of the Spirit. One can be engaged in meditating upon a passage while getting ready in the morning, while driving, throughout the day at work or home, in discussion with other believers, and when falling asleep at night—all while resting in the aid of the Spirit to enlighten the mind to the truth of the passage. One recommendation then is that when a particular truth is revealed in a moment of meditation, the student should have a system of jotting down those thoughts so that particular insights are not forgotten later during focused study of the passage.

As students ROAM, they will begin to move to the next step of inductive Bible study: interpretation, which is explored in the next chapter.

6

Interpreting and Generalizing the Text

Teach me good judgment and discernment,
for I rely on your commands.
—Psalm 119:66

In the apostle Paul's final letter in the Bible, he writes to a young protégé, Timothy, charging him to "Be diligent to present [himself] to God as one approved, a worker who doesn't need to be ashamed, correctly teaching the word of truth" (2 Tim 2:15). The "word of truth" that Timothy is to correctly teach is specifically the gospel, but also includes the entirety of God's Word. Paul tells Timothy that he should correctly handle the gospel and God's Word, and the phrase "correctly teach" in the original language speaks of "cutting straight," which is why some versions translate the phrase as "rightly dividing the Word." Timothy is instructed by Paul to be careful and precise in his teaching because the baton is being handed off as Paul entrusts Timothy with continuing the ministry of the Word. The command is a serious charge to every faithful expositor of God's Word, in particular pastor/elders who are tasked with preaching and teaching God's people. Yet, every believer who engages in teaching the Bible must also be careful and consider the weight of teaching the

Bible to others. One's philosophy of teaching God's Word should always include a commitment to handling the Scriptures with precise care.

In the last chapter, observation (the first step of the inductive method) was presented as a means to observe a Bible passage in such a way that the student asks the question, "What does the text say?" Once a student has observed a passage by "roaming" (Reading, writing down Observations, Asking questions, and Meditating) through it sufficiently, the student should begin the second step, which is interpretation, wherein the question is asked, "What does the text mean?" While observation promotes understanding, the step of interpretation pushes the student to discern the author's intended meaning for the original audience, so that she can then go on to the third step, which is generalizing the passage (stating the main idea of the passage and translating that main idea into a teaching idea). Thus, the step of observation builds the foundation for the work of interpretation, and the work of interpretation informs the construction of the main idea of the passage. The main idea then is translated into a focused teaching idea for one's audience.

In the previous section, we also discovered that four elements result in distance from the original passage for the modern reader (time, culture, language, and geography). In the same way, the presuppositions of the interpreter create distance when seeking to answer the question, "What does the text mean?" This chapter will explore the presuppositions of the interpreter, followed by four interpretive steps that, if followed, will render the ability to generalize the passage into one single statement leading to a focused teaching idea.

Presuppositions of the Interpreter

Presuppositions are beliefs or thoughts already in the mind of the interpreter that she brings with her from the moment she "roams" through a passage in observation through the four interpretive steps. Thus, before the student approaches the task of interpretation, she should consider how her presuppositions may influence her work in seeking out the author's intended meaning of a particular text. If we are able to identify our own preconceived notions, a cognizance about our own ways of thinking will promote the careful work of exegesis needed to discern the main idea of the text. Bill Curtis explains the importance of understanding presuppositions in *Engaging Exposition*:

> We all unavoidably bring presuppositions, biases, and preconceived ideas to the text. Kevin Vanhoozer rightly notes, "No one reads in a vacuum. Every reading is a contextualized reading." However, we are not bound to or enslaved by our presuppositions. They can be critiqued, altered, and even radically changed. An awareness of our presuppositions is an excellent starting point for doing honest, even humble, hermeneutics. Allowing them to be challenged is essential for doing good hermeneutics and exegesis.[1]

Curtis points out that interpreters should be aware of their own presuppositions. The question, then, is what particular viewpoints, theological beliefs, or worldviews does one hold that might create difficulty in arriving at the author's intended meaning? One may conclude that their own personal presuppositions—about postmodern philosophy (that meaning can be subjective), political ideologies, religious and theological background, the impact of one's cultural upbringing, commitments to gender-based issues, etc.—may color the search for meaning in a text. Only the reader knows where she stands on each area and how that area may impact her reading. But the truth that each reader approaches the Bible with certain preunderstandings of the interpretation of passages should be a fact that is kept in mind. Students should commit to a dogged determination to discern the main idea of the text as the author intended, knowing too that "with the assistance of the Spirit (His part) and by the means of proven principles of hermeneutics and exegesis (our part), we can grasp genuinely and truly, though not exhaustively, the wonderful truths of the Scriptures deposited by the Divine Author through human instruments."[2] Thus, understanding the role of preunderstandings, plus

---

[1] Akin, Curtis, and Rummage, *Engaging Exposition* (see chap. 1, n. 20), 36.
[2] Akin, Curtis, and Rummage, 36.

dependence upon the Holy Spirit, enables the student to be faithful in the next step, interpretation, and rightly dividing the Word.

Interpretation: Five Interpretive Steps

Since preunderstandings influence interpretation, before engaging with the five interpretive steps, consider the text and identify your preunderstandings:

- Jot down any particular interpretations of this passage that you have heard before (in sermons, teachings, books, etc.) that influence your current reading of it.
- Jot down any terms or ideas that seem "foreign" to you, that you might be likely to fill in with contemporary definitions or your own ideas. . . .
- Try to hear the passage and its message on its own terms as much as possible. Ask for God's guidance in this process.[3]

Once these three items are considered, work through interpreting the passage to get to the "MEATT" of the passage.

- **M** = Mine the Historical Background
- **E** = Examine the Context
- **A** = Analyze the Grammar
- **T** = Treasure the Genre
- **T** = Tie the Text to the Canon and Christ

Mine the Historical Background

The choice of the verb *mine* underscores that the task of understanding the history and culture surrounding a passage is an ongoing quest the Bible student undertakes. The reader must dig for information both inside and outside of the text (from other biblical texts which might

---

[3] Jeannine K. Brown, *Scripture as Communication: Introducing Biblical Hermeneutics* (Grand Rapids: Baker Academic, 2007), 276.

inform the reading of the particular text being studied, or from outside sources such as Bible dictionaries, encyclopedias, and commentaries).[4] First, to understand the historical background of any passage, the book being studied should be mined for clues as to why the author wrote the book. This information may have become clear while roaming through the passage. However, the following questions should be answered at this point if they have not already been considered:

- Who is the author of the book?
- Who is the audience/recipient of the book?
- Do any passages indicate the relationship between the author and the audience? If so, what is the relationship?
- What is the location of the author?
- What is his purpose for writing?
- What are the events surrounding the writing?

The answers to the questions above may be provided within the book of the Bible itself. Consider Galatians 1 and 2, where at least five of the six questions above are answered. In those two chapters, Paul identifies himself as the author, along with the recipients (the church at Galatia). He indicates the nature of his relationship with this church indirectly by speaking about his calling as an apostle to the Gentiles, and explains his purpose in writing when he skips over his traditional style of greetings/prayer to those he is writing to and indicates his astonishment that the Galatian church has abandoned the true gospel. Thus, the events surrounding the writing are clearly identifiable when he proclaims, "There are some who are troubling you and want to distort the gospel of Christ" (1:7). The text goes on to point out the distortion of the gospel related

---

[4] Reliable sources include commentaries that may be categorized as technical, pastoral, or devotional. In his pamphlet, "Building a Theological Library," Daniel L. Akin classifies technical commentaries as those that deal with the original languages, while pastoral commentaries are those written for the serious Bible student, pastor, or Bible teacher. A key distinctive for the third type, devotional commentaries, would be a focus on the text's application. Akin provides a helpful list of commentaries arranged according to the book of the Bible and tags each according to his classification.

to the Galatian church's pursuit of justification by works of the law (via circumcision, see 6:12), rather than justification by grace through faith in Christ. All of this information comes directly from an attentive reading of the book of Galatians.

Yet, the student should continue mining for more historical/cultural background of the text. Cross-referencing provides a rich system for digging into the backdrop of the text. For instance, in seeking to underscore the preeminent nature of God's grace in the gospel, Paul contrasts his current ministry with his past personal history, when he persecuted the church during his "former way of life in Judaism." Cross-references to that text lead to the book of Acts where one learns that Paul was a Pharisee. Students could continue using a cross-referencing system to understand Paul's "way of life" as a Pharisee but might also use a Bible dictionary for more information regarding Pharisaism. A study of this nature will increase the student's understanding of Galatians as Paul goes on to describe the hypocrisy of Christians who return to justification by the law.

Examine the Context

At this point in the study, the student should "confirm the limits of the passage . . . [and] become thoroughly acquainted with your paragraph/pericope."[5] The phrase, "limits of a passage," indicates that the teaching text should incorporate all the verses that incorporate a consistent, coherent unit of thought. During the first step of inductive study (observation), the limits of the passage may have been discerned through multiple readings of the text in different translations. If one has not determined all the verses that should be included in a lesson, the student should examine the context, which includes both the immediate verses and surrounding chapters.

Another element related to context is the passage's location within the entire book along with that book's place within Scripture. Be aware

---

[5] Fee, *New Testament Exegesis* (see chap. 5, n. 12), 35–36.

of the passage as it relates to the whole of the book and the whole of the Bible. The ability to discern the relationship between the particular passage and the book it is in prevents teaching a passage out of context. The key here is to understand the common practice of teaching Bible passages in a way that uses the text to present ideas unrelated to the actual progress of thought being made in the text as it relates to the whole. A common adage said among preachers and Bible teachers should be on the forefront of the mind when studying the Bible and when teaching: "A text without a context is a pretext for a proof text." (For more about proof-texting, refer to chapter 5 and the example from misuses of Phil 4:13.) Fuhr and Köstenberger call this type of teaching "interpretive malpractice," and note that many who do this may "do so because they have been trained (by example) to think through Scripture in terms of devotional nuggets, memorizing verses and reading for inspirational insight rather than interpretive understanding."[6] Of course, reading the Bible for devotion and inspiration, as well as memorizing it, are rewarding practices, however, devotional and inspirational thought derived from the Scriptures must find their foundation in the meaning of the text. Thus, commit to examining the context, allowing the interpretive meaning to be shaped by the author's intent.

Analyze the Grammar

This task may appear overwhelming, but with modern scholarship and the helps available to Bible students, along with a common knowledge of English grammar, the student has the ability to better interpret a passage by engaging with grammar in three ways:

1) *Identify independent clauses, dependent clauses, direct objects, and modifiers*—The words of a text make up sentences which signify an

---

[6] Fuhr Jr. and Köstenberger, *Inductive Bible Study* (see chap. 5, n. 6), 196.

author's proposition (his point or argument). To grasp the author's point, isolate key parts of a sentence:[7]

- *Independent clause*: has a subject + predicate; can stand alone by itself
- *Dependent clause*: typically introduced by a conjunction; cannot stand alone by itself
- *Direct object*: a noun phrase that receives the action of the verb (answers who or what)
- *Modifier*: can be a word, phrase, clause, or verb participle that acts either as an adjective or adverb and provides detail, information, or clarity

2) *Identify the verb tense*—For those who have not learned Greek, a basic knowledge of the six Greek verb tenses (present, imperfect, future, aorist, perfect, and pluperfect) can help a student with the meaning of the text, despite not knowing the original language. Various Bible softwares, apps, and websites identify the Greek verb tense, which informs the reader with the implications of the verb's tense:

- For both present and imperfect tenses—the action is "ongoing or in process, without attention to the action's beginning or ending"
- For both aorist and future tenses—the action is "complete or [portrayed] as a whole. The beginning and ending of the action (and everything in-between) are included in the depiction of the action"
- For both the perfect and pluperfect tenses—"the author depicts a state of affairs or ongoing relevance resulting from a previous action or state"[8]

---

[7] These four elements of a sentence may be easier to identify when diagramming a sentence. For an introduction to diagramming (in both Greek and English), see Benjamin L. Merkle and Robert L. Plummer, *Beginning with New Testament Greek: An Introductory Study of the Grammar and Syntax of the New Testament* (Nashville: B&H Academic, 2020), 231–33.

[8] Merkle and Plummer, *Beginning with New Testament Greek*, 41.

For example, consider Heb 4:14, which contains three verbs (underlined):

Therefore, since we <u>have</u> a great high priest who <u>has passed</u> through the heavens—Jesus the Son of God—<u>let us hold fast</u> to our confession.

One can use a website such as blueletterbible.org to determine the tense for each of these verbs:

- "Have"–Present Active
- "Has passed"–Perfect Active
- "Let us hold fast"–Present Active

Consider the implications of this verse: we presently and continually have a perfect high priest (Jesus, the Son of God); this great high priest has passed through the heavens in his ascension which is a previous action that has ongoing relevance for us; therefore, the writer encourages the reader, based upon these truths, to presently and continually hold fast to our confession.

3) *Identify and study significant words contained in the passage.* Fuhr and Köstenberger encourage that correct words should be chosen for a word study. Thus, they highlight six types of words for consideration:

- Contextual terms—"convey the primary argument or meaning of a passage"
- Theologically profound terms—"words or phrases that infer theological significance"
- Historically particular terms—"culturally, geographically, or historically particular terms that may not be understood outside of the world of the Bible"
- Exegetically uncertain terms—"words and phrases that are exegetically or textually uncertain in their context"
- Figurative terms—"words and phrases that convey figures of speech"
- Symbolic terms—"words and phrases that convey symbolic significance in a given context"[9]

---

[9] Fuhr Jr. and Köstenberger, *Inductive Bible Study*, 102.

The book of Jude is an excellent place to practice identifying the six types of terms listed above, as it contains all six types. Additionally, while doing word studies, also remember that a word contains a range of meaning, which is known as its "semantic range." (Refer to the previous discussion on the Greek word *gune*, which could mean either "woman" or "wife," depending on context.) When dealing with exegetically uncertain terms, one must seek to determine the particular meaning of a word in its use in a particular context to avoid what is known as a "word study fallacy." When a Bible teacher presents the full semantic range of a word as the word's meaning in the text, it is a word study fallacy, which happens "when a person imposes a significant portion or the totality of a word's semantic range into a single context."[10]

Thus, a word study must be boiled down to these three steps:

- identify the words for study
- discover the semantic range
- determine the meaning that fits the context

This section only briefly introduced concepts related to understanding the grammar of the Bible. Therefore, Bible students are encouraged to study the languages at a deeper level from a Greek or Hebrew scholar if possible.

Treasure the Literature

Remember the creativity of God and how his Word reflects both his creative nature and the personality of human writers of Scripture. Study the passage according to its particular genre (narrative, law, poetry, wisdom, prophecy, gospels, epistles, and apocalyptic) using the interpretive helps provided in chapter 3.[11]

---

[10] Fuhr Jr. and Köstenberger, 249. See also Benjamin L. Merkle, *Exegetical Gems from Biblical Greek: A Refreshing Guide* (Grand Rapids: Baker Academic, 2019).

[11] For additional help with the literature of the Bible, see *Introduction to Biblical Interpretation* by Klein, Blomberg, and Hubbard, as well as *How to Read the Bible for All Its Worth* by Fee.

After studying the text by walking through the four interpretive steps listed above, the meaning of the passage should come into focus. However, one final interpretive step must be considered before the meaning of the text can be articulated. Students should:

Tie the Text to the Canon and to Christ

This final step helps the Bible teacher to consider how the text *relates* to all of Scripture and *reveals* Jesus. The second interpretive step, "examine the context," concerned studying a Bible text as it relates to the book of the Bible in which it is found. However, if the Bible is unified, if there is an overarching storyline, and if the Bible has a main subject (underscored in chapter 2), then surely the student must consider where a particular text is located within the story and how it points to the main subject of the story, Jesus Christ.

To tie a text to the entire canon of Scripture, consider the time period of the particular text and where its contents fall within the history of the Bible:

- For an Old Testament text—Ask how the content points to or relates to the work of Jesus in the Gospels, the doctrines taught in the New Testament Epistles, and/or the hope of the consummation of all things in the book of Revelation. Readers will also want to ask if any New Testament writers quote or allude to the Old Testament text. If so, consider the consequence of how writers incorporated the Old Testament text into the New to inform interpretation. Additionally, readers should consider: in what ways does the life, death, burial, and/or ascension of Jesus fulfill this Old Testament text?

- For a New Testament text—Ask how the text might build upon themes first identified in the Old Testament. Consider how biblical writers have written about particular topics in other sections of the New Testament. For example, the apostle Paul writes about various subjects across several epistles. How does one instance of his writing shed light upon other portions of his writing? Beyond that, how might the entire New Testament or the entire Bible bring a fuller understanding of the meaning of the text at hand? Finally, how does the text point to the work of Christ?

Generalization

To this point, the inductive study method's first two steps have been covered: observation and interpretation. The next step is that of generalization, where the exegetical idea of the passage is identified and written down in a summarizing statement. The interpreter should gather all the details of the passage gleaned from observing and interpreting the passage to state the biblical author's thesis, point, or idea for a particular text concisely. Once the exegetical idea of the passage is determined and summarized, the teaching idea is then articulated.[12]

The Exegetical Idea

In general, to determine and state the exegetical idea, follow three steps: identify the passage subject, distinguish the passage complement, and write out the exegetical idea:

- *Identify the Passage Subject*—To identify the passage subject, one must answer the following question concerning the passage: what is the author talking about?
- *Determine the Passage Complement*—Determine the passage complement by asking, "What is the author saying about what

---

[12] Identifying the "passage subject" and the "passage complement" to form the exegetical idea comes from the work of Haddon W. Robinson. See *Biblical Preaching: The Development and Delivery of Expository Messages*, 3rd ed. (Grand Rapids: Baker Academic, 2014), 15–26. For examples of exegetical and teaching ideas for all of Scripture, see Matthew D. Kim and Scott M. Gibson, *The Big Idea Companion for Preaching and Teaching: A Guide from Genesis to Revelation* (Grand Rapids: Baker Academic, 2021).

he is talking about?" or "What is the author saying about the passage subject?"

- *State the Exegetical Idea*—Summarize the main idea of the passage in a single sentence by combining the passage subject and the passage complement:

Passage Subject + Passage Complement = Exegetical Idea

Consider the following example from Rom 5:1–5:

> Therefore, since we have been justified by faith, we have peace with God through our Lord Jesus Christ. We have also obtained access through him by faith into this grace in which we stand, and we boast in the hope of the glory of God. And not only that, but we also boast in our afflictions, because we know that affliction produces endurance, endurance produces proven character, and proven character produces hope. This hope will not disappoint us, because God's love has been poured out in our hearts through the Holy Spirit who was given to us.

- Passage subject (What is the author talking about?): The benefits of justification by faith for both Jews and Greeks (building upon the context of chapters 1–4 of Romans).
- Passage complement (What is the author saying about the passage subject?): That the benefits are: peace with God, access to God, and joy in affliction.
- Exegetical idea: Both Jews and Greeks, who have been justified by faith, have peace with God, have access to God, and have joy in affliction.

This method can also be applied to biblical narratives with slight modification:

- *Identify the Passage Subject*—To identify the passage subject, one must answer the following question concerning the passage: "What is the story about?"
- *Determine the Passage Complement*—Next, one determines the passage complement by asking, "What is being said through the story?"

- *State the Exegetical Idea*—Summarize the main idea of the passage in a single sentence by combining the passage subject and the passage complement.

Consider the following example from 2 Samuel 11 (which you are encouraged to read in its entirety). The passage recounts the story of David seeing Bathsheba, having her brought to him, him sleeping with her, her conception, and his deception and murder of her husband. The final verse of 2 Samuel says, "However, the Lord considered what David had done to be evil."

Passage subject (What is the story about?): David's sexual sin, deception, and murder.

Passage complement (What is being said through the story?): Sexual sin, deception, and murder was evil in God's eyes.

Exegetical idea: David's sexual sin, deception, and murder was evil in God's sight.

After the exegetical idea has been summarized, move on to state the "Teaching Idea."

The Teaching Idea

While the exegetical idea is a statement that articulates the point the biblical author made in the text, the teaching idea is a statement that the Bible teacher uses to connect or bridge the timeless principle of the text to a modern-day audience. The teaching idea must always stem from the exegetical idea of the passage, so that the teaching idea is located in the truth or argument that the biblical author sought to convey. Both exegetical ideas (from Rom 5:1–5 and 2 Samuel 11) are listed in the table below with a corresponding teaching idea.

Exegetical Idea	Teaching Idea
Both Jews and Greeks, who have been justified by faith, have peace with God, have access to God, and have joy in affliction.	Despite ethnicity or religious background, anyone who has been justified by faith has peace with God, access to God, and joy in affliction.
David's sexual sin, deception, and murder was evil in God's sight.	Believers can fall into great sin which brings displeasure to God.

One last word on the teaching idea and tying the text to the entire Bible and to Christ: consider that both teaching ideas listed above have canonical and Christological implications. In the interpretation section, the fifth step encouraged studying particular texts in light of the cohesive meta-narrative of the Scriptures and their Christ-centered nature. The teaching idea above for the passage about David and Bathsheba should find its conclusion in the grace of God in Christ. The text may be taught with Psalm 51 in mind and ultimately the redemption and salvation found in Christ for David's grievous sins—and the sins of believers.

After interpreting the text (by considering the five interpretive steps) and generalizing the text (by determining the exegetical idea and restating that idea in a teaching idea), the next steps of the inductive method follow: applying and implementing the text, which will be considered in the next chapter.

7

Applying and Implementing the Text

But be doers of the word and not hearers only, deceiving
yourselves. Because if anyone is a hearer of the word
and not a doer, he is like someone looking at his own
face in a mirror. For he looks at himself, goes away, and
immediately forgets what kind of person he was. But the
one who looks intently into the perfect law of freedom
and perseveres in it, and is not a forgetful hearer but a doer
who works—this person will be blessed in what he does.
—James 1:22–25

In the last two chapters, the first three steps of the inductive Bible study
method pointed the student to consider what the text says (observation), what the text means (interpretation), and how the main idea of the
passage should be stated (generalization). Yet, the process of hermeneutics would be incomplete if one were to stop thinking through the text
after engaging with the first three steps. The very nature of the Bible
(see chapter 1) compels the exegete to consider ways that the Word of
God speaks for the believer today, thus finding "meaningful connections

between the passage and contemporary living."[1] Since the Bible is God's Word (being inspired, infallible, inerrant, authoritative, sufficient, clear, and necessary) the very words of Scripture not only must be interpreted correctly, but they must also be applied and implemented consistently in the life of the believer.

This truth is seen clearly in Jas 1:22–25, where Christians are instructed to not just hear the word, but to "be doers of the word" (v. 22). However, one cannot properly obey James's command to be a "doer of the word" without first understanding the surrounding context of verse 22. James 1 offers a progression to the work of God's Word in the life of a believer, which begins with salvation. James 1:18 says, "By his own choice, he [God] gave us birth by the word of truth so that we would be a kind of firstfruits of his creatures." This verse teaches that people are born again by God's choice and through his Word, which is a theme consistent with the entirety of the Bible. For instance, 1 Pet 1:23 points to the role of Scripture in salvation, ". . . you have been born again—not of perishable seed but of imperishable—through the living and enduring word of God." In 1:25, Peter goes on to specifically define the "word" as "the gospel that was proclaimed to you," reminding us that salvation comes through the Word of Christ, through whom we are redeemed. Therefore, as James instructs Christians to be obedient to God's Word, he roots that obedience in the new birth that comes about by God's own choice and will, through "the word of truth" or rather, the Scriptures and the proclamation of the gospel. Then, James goes on to teach that God's Word has been implanted in those who have been born again by the Word in 1:21, which states, "Therefore, ridding yourselves of all moral filth and the evil that is so prevalent, humbly receive the implanted word, which is able to save your souls." Regarding this verse, Douglas Moo comments upon the phrase "receive the implanted word":

> . . . implanted in you is not a command to unbelievers to be converted ("accept the word" means this elsewhere in the New Testament), but to believers to allow the word to influence them

---

[1] Richards and Bredfeldt, *Creative Bible Teaching* (see chap. 1, n. 9), 75.

in all parts of their lives. By adding the word *humbly* to the command, James reminds us that we need to be open and receptive to the work of the word in the heart. Christians who have truly been "born again" (v. 18) demonstrate that the word has transformed them by their humble acceptance of that word as their authority and guide for life.[2]

At this point, James then gives the command: "But be doers of the word and not hearers only, deceiving yourselves." The progression of thought is that believers are born again "by the word of truth" resulting in God's Word being implanted within them that they are to "humbly receive." Consequently, they are to be doers of God's Word. So the warning from James is this: those who only listen to God's Word but do not obey it—these people are deceiving themselves into thinking they are Christians when they are not, for true Christians not only hear God's Word but are equipped by the Spirit to obey God's implanted Word.

Jesus taught this exact concept in the parable he gave on the sower. In Mark 4:1–20, Jesus tells an illustrative story about a sower who sowed seed in four different types of ground: along a path, upon rocky ground, amidst thorns, and on good ground. The seed sown on the path, the rocky ground, and among the thorns did not bear any lasting fruit—only the good ground produced fruit that "increased thirty, sixty, and a hundred times" (Mark 4:8). When the twelve disciples ask Jesus in private to explain the parable, he tells them that the four types of ground represent four types of people and their response to the seed of God's Word:

1. The seed sown along the path illustrates the type of person who hears the Word, but the Word sown in them is stolen away by Satan (v. 15)
2. The seed sown upon the rocky ground reveals that there are persons who hear the Word and receive it with joy, but they are only temporarily rooted in the Word and fall away when facing hardship or enduring persecution (vv. 16–17)

---

[2] Douglas J. Moo, *The Pillar New Testament Commentary: The Letter of James* (Grand Rapids: Eerdmans, 2000), 87–88.

3. The seed sown amidst the thorns pictures those who also hear the Word, but the Word is choked out by the worries of the world, the deceitfulness of wealth, or desires for other things, causing the Word to be unfruitful (vv. 18–19)

4. The seed sown on good ground portrays those who hear the Word, welcome the Word, and produce fruit (v. 20)

The mark of a true Christian is one who hears, welcomes, and, empowered by the Holy Spirit, produces fruit consistent with God's Word. A true Christian bears the fruit of the Spirit and not only continually seeks to listen to or hear what the Scriptures say, but desires to put all of God's Word into practice. Thus, the next two steps of application and implementation of the inductive method (as articulated by Richards and Bredfeldt) complete the entire process for which the Bible teacher studies: growth in godliness and conformity to the image of Christ.

The following sections introduce both applying the text and implementing the text. However, the first three steps of observation, interpretation, and generalization cannot be overemphasized. These three steps lay the foundation for how a text is applied personally and put into practice in daily life. Bible teachers sometimes read a text and jump to ideas they have about how the text applies without first thinking through the original intent of the author and the meaning the passage held for the original recipient. Thus, one must consider the following rule when discerning ways that a text may be applied and implemented:

> Interpretation always precedes application. Application should be rooted in the central principle taught in the text. In fact, application of a passage cannot and should not be made apart from careful interpretation of the passage. The question, "What difference does it make?" is a legitimate one, but we must exercise care here that we do not make a passage say what it does not say.[3]

While interpretation must always precede application, one should be aware of two possible extremes when teaching the text. Gary Newton

---

[3] Richards and Bredfeldt, *Creative Bible Teaching*, 71.

notes that these two extremes come when teachers "either . . . try to teach their students exactly what they learned from the text for themselves; or, in an attempt to relate to students' needs, they stray from the original intent of the text. Both extremes fail to do justice to the nature of Scripture and the nature of the student. Teachers must exegete accurately both Scripture and the student."[4] Thus, when teachers seek to help listeners apply the text and implement the text, he suggests that they "put themselves in the role of their students as they reflect on the biblical text. Teachers need to hypothesize what the students might be thinking, feeling, experiencing, struggling with, frustrated with, happy about, or anticipating while they are reading the text."[5]

The next two sections consider the next two steps of applying the text and implementing the text while remaining committed to the exegetical idea and the type of student who will make up the audience for the lesson presentation.

Applying the Text

The previous chapter noted that the grammatical-historical method teaches that a text has one meaning and that the exegete works to uncover a text's meaning through an established hermeneutical process (using the inductive Bible study method). A common adage is that while a text has one meaning, it can have many applications. The teacher of God's Word should spend significant time thinking through ways the text at hand applies to the life of the learner. This section recommends asking questions to personally apply the text, followed by the biblical paradigm for application, as well as using the great commandment as a grid for application. Finally, the section ends by drawing upon educational theory to help one contemplate applying the Bible to the entire person.

---

[4] Gary Newton, *Heart-Deep Teaching: Engaging Students for Transformed Lives* (Nashville: B&H Academic, 2012), 85.

[5] Newton, 88.

As noted above, the work of application begins with asking the following question of the text: "What difference does it make?"[6] The Christian must always ask the question, "Why has this Word been preserved and what is its implication for me personally?" Why ask these questions? As Piper notes, "The aim of biblical writers is not only that we know things, but that we do things and do them in a certain way. So part of our response to Scripture is to form the habit of asking questions concerning application—to ourselves, our church and other Christians, to our relationships, to our culture, to the unbelievers and institutions of the world. This means that the task of application is never done."[7]

Thus, questions of application must be considered because God works through his Word in a very personal way, according to Hebrews 4. The Bible teaches that God's Word lays bare the thoughts and intentions of the heart, exposing his creatures: "For the word of God is living and effective and sharper than any double-edged sword, penetrating as far as the separation of soul and spirit, joints and marrow. It is able to judge the thoughts and intentions of the heart. No creature is hidden from him, but all things are naked and exposed to the eyes of him to whom we must give an account" (Heb 4:12–13). When the teacher of the Word has studied a text by observing, interpreting, and generalizing it, she must then enter into the process of assessing how the text functions to bring about personal change in her own life, in her own thoughts and intentions. She must prayerfully seek God's help to see how the Scripture might make a difference for her individually. Kay Arthur provides helpful questions to consider when seeking to think through personal application:

1. How does the meaning of this passage apply to me?
2. What truths am I to embrace, believe, or order my life by?
3. What changes should I make in my belief, in my life?[8]

---

[6] Richards and Bredfeldt, *Creative Bible Teaching*, 71.

[7] John Piper, *Reading the Bible Supernaturally: Seeing and Savoring the Glory of God in Scripture* (Wheaton, IL: Crossway, 2017), 379.

[8] Kay Arthur, *How to Study Your Bible: The Lasting Rewards of the Inductive Method* (Eugene, OR: Harvest House Publishers, 1994), 111.

Once a student has considered personal application, she should then contemplate how the text might apply for those she intends to teach. Thus, the Bible teacher must consider how a specific text might be used by the Holy Spirit to bring about sanctification in the life of believers. Since the Bible is given by inspiration of the Spirit, we also know that it is useful for teaching believers, for rebuking their sin, for correcting them in any way that is contrary to God's Word, and for training them in righteousness (godly living). Paul reveals these truths in 2 Tim 3:16–17: "All Scripture is inspired by God and is profitable for teaching, for rebuking, for correcting, for training in righteousness, so that the man of God may be complete, equipped for every good work." Based upon this verse, a pattern for application is discerned, where the teacher can ask questions according to the four benefits of the Bible outlined by the apostle Paul, who says the Bible is useful for:

- Teaching—does the passage identify a particular doctrine to be learned and followed?
- Rebuking—does this passage communicate a reproof for sin(s) that need to be explained, leading to repentance?
- Correcting—does the passage highlight ways a belief or practice should be corrected?
- Training in righteousness—in what ways does this passage point to the righteousness of Christ in the place of the believer or in what ways does it train the Christian for godly living?[9]

While 2 Tim 3:16–17 offers a helpful standard to follow, another Scriptural paradigm for application may be discerned from Jesus's teaching on the Great Commandment. In Mark 12:28–30, a scribe of the law questions Jesus:

> "Which command is the most important of all?" Jesus answered, "The most important is 'Listen, Israel! The Lord our God, the Lord is one. *Love the Lord your God with all your heart, with all*

---

[9] Richards and Bredfeldt, *Creative Bible Teaching*, 96–97.

your soul, with all your mind, and with all your strength" (emphasis added).

The command that Jesus identifies as the most important relates to one's relationship with God and how believers are to love God with the entirety of their being: with the heart, soul, mind, and strength. Thus, when thinking through the application of any particular text, a Bible teacher could ask how the Scripture pushes one to love God according to the four areas Jesus identified:

- With all one's heart—how does this passage help me to love God with my emotions and desires?
- With all one's soul—in what ways does this passage teach me about my relationship with the Lord?
- With all one's mind—how does this passage help renew my mind with new thought patterns? Does it contain specific doctrine that I should study more in-depth?
- With all one's strength—what does this passage teach me about using my body for God's glory?[10]

The Great Commandment considered above lends to the idea that biblical application should be determined by the four categories of heart, soul, mind, and strength, yet traditional educational categories may also be contemplated. William Yount, a long-time professor who specializes in Christian education, developed the "Christian teacher's triad" to help teachers think through the makeup of human beings as they are involved in lesson planning. Educational theory points out that human beings are thinkers, feelers, and doers, and thus should be instructed according to the three following learning domains: cognitive (mind), affective (emotions), and behavioral (doing). Yount incorporates the three learning domains to encourage teaching to the entire person, so that the Bible teacher might ask:

---

[10] For more about loving the Lord holistically in these ways, see Kristin L. Kellen and Julia B. Higgins, *The Whole Woman: Ministering to Her Heart, Soul, Mind, and Strength* (Nashville: B&H, 2021).

- *Thinking (Cognitive)*—How does this text cause a person to grow in understanding and knowledge, and critically assess beliefs concerning God?
- *Feeling (Affective)*—How does this text cause a person to consider their emotions, attitudes, and values in light of glorifying God?
- *Doing (Behavioral)*—In what ways does this text encourage a person to correct their behavior?

Thus, as a teacher prepares lessons, they can utilize the Christian teacher's triad to intentionally apply biblical texts. Yet, in all the ways mentioned above that enable a Bible student to think through applying the Scriptures, Kay Arthurs's three areas of warning should be heeded. She states, "When applying Scripture, beware of the following: 1) Applying cultural standards rather than biblical standards; 2) Attempting to strengthen a legitimate truth by using a Scripture incorrectly; 3) Applying Scripture out of prejudice from past training or teaching."[11]

With the above suggested means of applying a text, let's consider an example from Rom 5:1–5, which says:

> Therefore, since we have been justified by faith, we have peace with God through our Lord Jesus Christ. We have also obtained access through him by faith into this grace in which we stand, and we boast in the hope of the glory of God. And not only that, but we also boast in our afflictions, because we know that affliction produces endurance, endurance produces proven character, and proven character produces hope. This hope will not disappoint us, because God's love has been poured out in our hearts through the Holy Spirit who was given to us.

For the sake of illustration, imagine that the first three steps of the inductive method have been completed, resulting in a generalizing statement (boiling down the ideas of the passage into one sentence) which constitutes the exegetical idea:

---

[11] Arthur, *How to Study Your Bible*, 115.

Both Jews and Greeks who have been justified by faith have peace with God, have access to God, and have joy in affliction.

This exegetical idea was identified in chapter 6, as well the teaching idea that bridges the timeless principle of the text for a modern-day audience:

Despite ethnicity or religious background, anyone who has been justified by faith has peace with God, access to God, and joy in affliction.

At this point, the exegete must contemplate the passage for personal application as well as for corporate application for those she will teach. With the suggested personal application questions in mind, a student might consider the following answers:

1. *How does the meaning of this passage apply to me?* The exegete might think through her personal salvation story and how it has brought about actual peace with and access to God. She might contemplate times where she has experienced joy in affliction, because she has seen affliction produce endurance, character, and hope in her walk with God.

2. *What truths am I to embrace, believe, or order my life by?* She may consider embracing the idea that the Christian life is not one free from affliction; rather when afflictions arise, she can reorient her mind to believe that when afflictions arise, benefits come, which include endurance, character, and hope in God.

3. *What changes should I make in my belief, in my life?* Since the text teaches that justification has brought peace with and access to God, she should repent of any fleeing from God when sin arises, but rather should run toward God knowing that justification is hers by faith in Christ who has been perfect in her place.

Regarding application for a particular teaching audience, the teacher might contemplate ways the passage enables listeners to love God with their whole heart (emotions, desires), soul (their relationship with the Lord), mind (doctrinally, renewed thought patterns), and strength (with their body). Just as personal application brought about her own personal testimony, she might help others to love God with their soul by sharing what justification is, leading also to a discussion on the doctrine of justification. She might also help listeners think through patterns of thought about fleeing from God rather than running to him when sin takes place, so that she might understand the access and peace she has been granted through justification by faith. Additionally, when using 2 Tim 3:16–17 as a paradigm, two of the four categories may be helpful, in that she may consider how the passage is useful for teaching (on the doctrine of justification) as well as for training in righteousness (encouraging godly living by promoting an understanding of hoping in God in the midst of affliction, resulting in endurance and proven character).

Implementing the Text

While the last section considered the idea that there are many applications of a text, this section concerns ways that one can put Scripture into practice. One might ask, "What does it mean to *implement* a text?" Most inductive methods center upon applying the text (which might include the thought of obeying a text), but the word *implement* highlights that one can apply the text personally without necessarily tangibly obeying the text. Thus, to implement a text means to carry it out, to obey it, to do it, to accomplish something. While application asks, "What difference does it make?" with a view toward introspection, implementation asks, "What must I change?" causing the Bible student to consider how the text may be obeyed concretely. Therefore, "it is important that as readers of the Bible we do not merely approach the Word of God as information to be learned, but as life changing truth meant to transform us."[12]

This transformation takes place over the course of one's life after they are initially converted to follow Christ. The apostle John often notes how implementing the words of Scripture in one's life reveals that one has truly been born again. In John 14:21, he quotes Jesus as saying, "The one who has my commands and keeps them is the one who loves me."

---

[12] Richards and Bredfeldt, *Creative Bible Teaching*, 77.

John reiterates the truth Jesus conveyed in John 14:21 in the epistle of 1 John as well:

> This is how we know that we know him: if we keep his commands. The one who says, "I have come to know him," and yet doesn't keep his commands, is a liar, and the truth is not in him. But whoever keeps his word, truly in him the love of God is made complete. This is how we know we are in him: The one who says he remains in him should walk just as he walked. (1 John 2:3–6)

Thus, John concludes near the end of the epistle: "For this is what love for God is: to keep his commands. And his commands are not a burden, because everyone wo has been born of God conquers the world. This is the victory that has conquered the world: our faith" (1 John 5:3–4). In these three different portions of Scripture, John consistently teaches that keeping God's commands offers a proof of salvation and love for God. This concept relates to what was already seen in the first section, that applying and implementing a text must be rooted in the truths taught in James 1 (people are born again by the Word of God, leading to God implanting his Word in the believers, resulting in their ability to be doers of the Word) and Mark 4 (that those who hear the Word and welcome it bear much fruit). But notice the phrase "and his commands are not a burden" in 1 John 5. This expression should highlight a particular truth for the Bible teacher to be aware of when thinking through ways to help students put a Scripture into practice. The teacher of God's Word must find ways to implement the text (to obey the Scripture) that are based in the gospel of grace rather than works-based righteousness. Kistemaker, in his commentary on 1 John, remarks that "the Pharisees and scribes placed unnecessary demands upon the Jewish people of the first century. They added to the decalogue hundreds of manmade rules that were burdensome to the people."[13] So while the warning may be made that a Bible teacher must not push for putting something into practice

---

[13] Simon J. Kistemaker, *New Testament Commentary: Exposition of the Epistles of John* (Grand Rapids: Baker Books, 1986), 349.

that goes beyond what the text is teaching, following in the footsteps of the Pharisees and scribes, one must hold tightly to the aforementioned thought that obedience to God's commands reveals that true conversion has taken place in the life and heart of the one who has professed Christ. This causes some tension because the one who teaches does not in any way want to lay extrabiblical demands upon believers (and by doing so, in some way convey that salvation depends upon faith plus works) but should be committed to teaching the entirety of a text, which includes commands from God himself (and that true faith is demonstrated by works). The solution, then, to this tension must be for the teacher to reflect upon the commands of the text in light of how each command has been accomplished through the person and work of Christ, rooting Christian obedience to a text in positional righteousness.

For example, many New Testament epistles follow the exact pattern mentioned above, that of locating one's ability to obey in one's identity in Christ. This form is articulated by offering first doctrinal sections followed by passages concerning the ethics of the Christian life. Ephesians is often provided as an illustration of this concept: chapters 1–3 provide a basis for who one is in Christ, and chapters 4–6 then give instruction on how to live out that calling, marked by the transitional statement from Paul, "Therefore I, the prisoner in the Lord, urge you to walk worthy of the calling you have received." Paul then goes on to offer many commands, such as:

- Take off your former way of life and put on your new self (Eph 4:22–24)
- Put away lying and speak the truth (Eph 4:25)
- Be angry and do not sin (Eph 4:26)
- Be kind and compassionate, forgiving one another (Eph 4:32)

Each of these commands are to be implemented in the life of the Christian, but are rooted in the fact that a believer in Christ is one who is a new person "created according to God's likeness in righteousness and purity of the truth" (Eph 4:24). Thus, the teacher should always look for ways to implement the text that roots obedience to it in the righteousness that is the believer's based upon the merits of Christ. Looking for connections to positional righteousness will prevent a moralistic tone in teaching implementation. Practically, a teacher should call people to speak truth and quit lying or forsake anger and replace anger with kindness, compassion, and forgiveness (first by way of personal, inward application in repentance) but also by calling for practical implementation in areas of life where believers walk in the sins of lying, anger, and unforgiveness.

In the book, *Grasping God's Word*, the authors provide a three-step process for application that is helpful for thinking through ways to apply and implement a text:

1. Observe how the principles in the text address the original situation.
2. Discover a parallel situation in a contemporary context.
3. Make your applications specific.[14]

This step will be reiterated and explored further in chapter 8. However, as one contemplates applying and implementing a biblical text, Rom 8:29 provides rich encouragement that the work of salvation and sanctification will be completed for those in Christ, because, as Paul states, "For those he foreknew he also predestined to be conformed to the image of his Son, so that he would be the firstborn among many brothers and sisters" (Rom 8:29).

---

[14] J. Scott Duvall and J. Daniel Hays, *Grasping God's Word: A Hands-On Approach to Reading, Interpreting, and Applying the Bible* (Grand Rapids: Zondervan Academic, 2020), 244–47.

8

From Study to Presentation

Just as each one has received a gift, use it to serve others, as
good stewards of the varied grace of God. If anyone speaks,
let it be as one who speaks God's words; if anyone serves,
let it be from the strength God provides, so that God may
be glorified through Jesus Christ in everything. To him
be the glory and the power forever and ever. Amen.
—1 Peter 4:10–11

One of my favorite lines from a Christian rap artist comes from Shai
Linne, on his album entitled, *The Church: Called and Collected*. Linne
defines and explains various marks of a church through his lyrical gifting
on his record, with my favorite line coming from his rap, "Expositional
Preaching." The song's lyrics push the listener to consider the type of
preaching they hear in church, explaining the necessity and importance
for pastors to faithfully exegete a text for a congregation and apply the
Scripture within its context. The line that stands out most is when Shai
Linne asks the listener to consider: "Was the point of the passage the
point of the sermon?"

The question underscores the idea that someone might engage in the
hard work of exposition to get to the main idea of the text and might hold

to a belief in the need for expository preaching, yet could preach or teach in a way that fails to explain the exegetical idea that was discovered during the inductive process. Due to such a possibility, the theme of the next few chapters is to build upon the first section, which concerned principles of teaching. To this point, the first section covered the steps that a Bible teacher works through to discern the meaning of a passage and how to put the passage into practice: observing, interpreting, generalizing, applying, and implementing. The five inductive steps, thus, build the foundation for teaching the Bible in a way that includes the main idea of the author for the intended audience while also applying and implementing the text for the modern reader in the circumstances that are distinct from that of the biblical audience yet are very much applicable to and sufficient for life and godliness in the world today.

This chapter, then, explicitly concerns taking the foundational elements of inductive Bible study to build a lesson for the purpose of teaching women the Bible expositionally. While Linne's question in his rap was written about pastoral preaching, it should be the driving question for any person committed to teaching the Bible to others. Discerning the exegetical idea and teaching and applying the Scriptures according to the main point of the passage applies to every Christian not only as they read the Bible for themselves but also as they seek to teach and disciple other believers.

In the introduction of this book, the idea of promoting a pathway for women to exercise teaching gifts in the local church was presented. The introduction noted that pastors have been given the responsibility to shepherd a church, protect the doctrine of the body, and manage the discipleship processes according to the needs of the local church. Titus 1 and 2 provides a descriptive account of the apostle Paul appointing a church planter, Titus, to appoint overseers or pastors in Crete (Titus 1:5). Paul then goes on to instruct Titus that women of the church are to be involved in the task of discipling other women. The concluding application from Paul's letter to Titus is that pastors must be aware of their responsibility to promote gender specific discipleship in their local church. Additionally, the introduction of the book discussed the idea that women, alongside their brothers in Christ, have been commissioned by Jesus to go and make disciples, teaching them to observe all that he commanded; and the truth that women have also been empowered by the Holy Spirit with varying spiritual gifts was underscored.

While women have been commissioned by Jesus to share the gospel and teach others to observe all that he has commanded, and while Titus 2 reveals that women are to specifically be about the task of discipling other women, a continued discussion on how the Bible teaches about spiritual gifts will aid those who seek to teach. This chapter began by quoting 1 Pet 4:10–11, a text that concerns spiritual gifts. In 1 Peter, the apostle Peter tells the recipients of his letter (those whom he has identified in 1:1 as "those chosen, living as exiles dispersed abroad") to use their gift "to serve others, as good stewards of the varied grace of God. If anyone speaks, let it be as one who speaks God's words. . . ." This Scripture points to the purpose and use of spiritual gifts, mainly that each believer has been given "a varied grace" from God that is to be stewarded appropriately—a spiritual gift was given to each believer by God that each might serve others. Tom Schreiner, in his commentary on 1 Peter, speaks to this thought:

> The point is that spiritual gifts are given to serve and to help others, to strengthen others in the faith. They are bestowed for ministry, not to enhance self-esteem. Paul emphasized the same theme, reminding believers that gifts are given to build up and edify others, not to edify oneself (1 Cor 12:7, 25–26; 14:1–19, 26; Eph 4:11–12). When believers use their gifts to strengthen others, they are functioning as "good stewards" (NRSV, *kaloi oikonomoi*) of God's grace. The word translated "stewards" could also be translated as "managers" (cf. Luke 12:42; 16:1, 3, 8; 1 Cor 4:1–2; cf. Gal 4:2; Titus 1:7), as long as it is clear that believers hold these gifts in trust since they are gifts of God. Spiritual gifts are not fundamentally a privilege but a responsibility, a call to be faithful to what God has bestowed.[1]

---

[1] Schreiner, *New American Commentary: 1, 2 Peter, Jude* (see chap. 1, n. 13), 214.

Thus, not only are women commanded to fulfill the Great Commission and are called to disciple women in the local church, they are instructed to faithfully use their spiritual gifts to serve others. They are to manage their gifts with the understanding that the Holy Spirit blessed them in particular ways for the upbuilding, edification, and service of the local church. With this in mind, consider how 1 Pet 4:10 goes on to say, "If anyone speaks, let it be as one who speaks God's words. . . ." Along with Romans 12, which mentions a teaching gift, this text highlights those who have been given speaking gifts, offering specific instruction on how that speaking gift should be expressed:

> Those who speak should endeavor to speak "the very words of God." . . . Using speaking gifts to minister to others means that the one speaking endeavors to speak God's words. How easy it is to think that we can assist others with our own wisdom, but those who are entrusted with the ministry of speaking should be careful to speak God's words, to be faithful to the gospel (cf. 1 Cor 4:1–2; 2 Tim 4:1–5).[2]

Those who teach should be vigilant, then, to speak truthfully and in keeping with what God has said in his Word. While the exegetical process discerns the meaning of the text, those who have teaching and speaking gifts must commit to crafting messages that lay bare the meaning of the text they are teaching and help listeners to understand ways they can apply and implement God's Word in their lives. This chapter will introduce the "hook, book, look, took" method, which can be modified to incorporate small group discussion.

The HBLT Method

In their book, *Creative Bible Teaching*, Richards and Bredfeldt not only identify five steps to the inductive Bible study method (observation, interpretation, generalization, application, and implementation), but

---

[2] Schreiner, 215.

they also present four memorable words that allow for the Bible teacher to organize studied material into a teaching outline.[3] The four words (hook, book, look, took) provide a simple path for a teacher to write a lesson, Bible curriculum, or presentation to teach the Bible in an expository manner that holds to presenting the main idea of the text while also allowing for dialogue, an element that lends to Bible teaching rather than preaching. The HBLT method offers one way for teachers to accomplish that task. The first step, then, is to "hook" your audience.

Hook

Handbooks on public speaking typically include the idea that listeners decide in the first 10–30 seconds whether or not they will listen to a speech. While teaching God's Word is not like a speech one might present to business colleagues or in a public speaking class, teachers might consider the way they can engage the listener to better hear and understand the message. Thus, a memorable quote, story, statistic, question, or even appropriate joke may prove beneficial in piquing the interest of the audience, effectively "hooking" the listener so that she desires to hear what will be said, recognizes the need for attentive listening on her part, and is receptive to the content that follows the hook. Since a hook is incorporated to ensure a listener's engagement, the Bible teacher should take care in crafting it.

Therefore, the key to a good hook is to make sure the device that is chosen grabs the attention of the learner. Beyond that, a good hook is relevant to the passage and does not distract from the passage. Additionally, it should be the appropriate length and set the stage for diving into the text in a meaningful way. Think about sermons and Bible lessons you have heard in the past. Speakers who are skilled at offering an engaging introduction use their creativity to find relatable, present-day oriented information to connect the modern ear to the teachings of the ancient Scriptures. A specific way to accomplish that connection is to plan and

---

[3] See Richards and Bredfeldt, *Creative Bible Teaching* (see chap. 1, n. 9), 171–73.

write out the hook, which then includes a transitional statement that links the story or quote to the exact idea of the biblical text. Also, the hook should not be extremely long but should be long enough to grab the attention of listeners—but not too long where listeners' attention will begin to drift or become frustrated. One way to gauge how long the hook should be is to apply a simple formula: the number of total minutes of speaking time multiplied by 10 percent. For example, if the allotment of speaking time is forty minutes, the hook should last no longer than four minutes.

For an example of a hook, consider a lesson on Revelation 4. This text is a magnificent passage that conveys a vision of God on his throne that the apostle John received when he was invited to enter into God's throne room as he was caught up in the Spirit (Rev 4:1–2). Through the use of imagery, the language of the chapter captures the many attributes of God as he is presented as seated on a throne. If one were teaching on this text, she might use a "hook" to help the listener consider the wonder of the vision that John receives and writes down, a vision that God has preserved in his Word for believers so they might have a glimpse of the Almighty in all of his glory. One way to increase this wonder would be to first highlight how human beings truly desire to know what heaven is going to be and look like, using an example from culture. Then, the teacher could connect that desire to know about heaven to the fact that the Bible gives us all we need to know about heaven, mainly that God and his throne are at the center and are the main focus of heavenly activity. Consider an example of how this hook might be written:

> Many years ago, a three-year-old boy named Colton had a near-death experience in a hospital on an operating room table. When he awoke after surgery, Colton told his parents how he went to heaven and saw Jesus, John the Baptist, and his own grandfather, and he told of all that he had experienced while he was there. You might recognize Colton as the little boy from a *New York Times* best-seller called, *Heaven Is for Real.* The popularity of this book cannot be understated—over 11 million copies have been sold, and the book was on the *New York Times* best seller list for

ten weeks. On top of the book sales, Hollywood made a movie about Colton's story, which grossed 101.3 million dollars in the United States. The widespread fame of this story and those who capitalized on it for profit reveals one thing to us: people are so incredibly interested in knowing what will happen after they die that they will seek out ways to gain a better understanding from anyone who has claimed to have been to heaven and come back, even if that means paying to hear the story from a three-year-old. Obviously, people want to know what heaven is like, for the Bible teaches us that eternity has been written on our hearts! This longing to understand and know is a part of our makeup as human beings. The question, then, is not should we seek out resources on heaven, but to which resources do we go? I'm here to tell you today that we have an extremely reliable source on what heaven is like, written down by the apostle John himself. Before John died, he was invited to see God on his throne in the book of Revelation—he was given a true vision from God, and we are invited to peer into the throne room with him, in Revelation, chapter 4.

This example provides a current, real-life example that taps into the universal experience of wonder about the afterlife, while also encouraging the listener to consider that the Bible is the ultimate source for that information. The hook compels the listener to then consider a specific text, hopefully speaking to their heart and emotions, drawing them in to learn from the book from a cognitive standpoint, transitioning smoothly into an inductive examination of the text.

Book

The book section consists of the teacher and listener engaging in an in-depth study of the particular text that was identified in the hook. The teacher should craft this section based upon the observation, interpretation, and generalization steps, while walking the listener through the Scripture, verse-by-verse. The preferred method for expository teaching differs from one person to the next according to various philosophies on how exegesis is done. Tony Merida highlights the diverse definitions (and interpretations) of expository preaching in his book *The Christ-Centered Expositor.*[4] The last two definitions he lists provide the necessary information for a complete understanding of exposition:

- Merida quotes Vines and Shaddix from their book, *Power in the Pulpit:* "[An expository sermon is] a discourse that expounds a passage of Scripture, organizes it around a central theme and main divisions which issue forth the given text, and then decisively applies its message to the listeners."[5]
- Merida quotes D. A. Carson from a talk he gave at a pastors conference: "At its best, expository preaching is preaching which, however dependent it may be for its content, upon text(s) at hand, draws attention to inner-canonical connections (connections within Scripture) that inexorably moves to Jesus Christ."[6]

These two descriptions of what expository preaching involves encapsulate what Bible teachers should also seek to accomplish when teaching, especially during the book portion of the lesson. The book section should contain an exposition of the Scripture, which is organized by the text's main idea and the natural divisions within the text, while seeking to interpret the text within the larger context of the Bible (highlighting ways the particular text relates to all of the Bible) with an aim toward presenting Christ to the listener. Typically, expository preaching provides the background information of the text (the book's author, purpose and theme along with the immediate context surrounding the particular text being studied), and then seeks to walk the listener through an outline of the text, where every verse (and phrases within those verses) unveils for the listener the text's meaning that was presented as a proposition to

---

[4] Tony Merida, *The Christ-Centered Expositor: A Field Guide for Word-Driven Disciple Makers* (Nashville: B&H Academic, 2016), 14–15.

[5] Jerry Vines and Jim Shaddix, *Power in the Pulpit* (Chicago: Moody, 1999), 29.

[6] D. A. Carson, "The Primacy of Expository Preaching," Bethlehem Conference for Pastors, 1995, cassette.

the listener. Often, teachers use illustrations to further demonstrate the meaning of the text and to provide meaningful connection for the listener.

Consider an example of the book portion from a lesson on Heb 4:14–16, which says:

> Therefore, since we have a great high priest who has passed through the heavens—Jesus the Son of God—let us hold fast to our confession. For we do not have a high priest who is unable to sympathize with our weaknesses, but one who has been tempted in every way as we are, yet without sin. Therefore, let us approach the throne of grace with boldness, so that we may receive mercy and find grace to help us in time of need.

After doing an inductive study of this particular text, the exegetical idea and the teaching idea have been determined through the generalization step as follows:

Exegetical Idea	Teaching Idea
The knowledge of Jesus as great high priest was meant to propel the recipients of the book of Hebrews to hold fast to their confession of faith and to boldly approach God for help.	For believers, the knowledge of Jesus as our great high priest propels us to hold fast to our confession and approach God in times of need.

While the exegetical idea simply states the main idea of the text in one sentence, the teaching idea builds off of the exegetical idea to help the listener apply the text personally. Thus, in building a lesson on Heb 4:14–16, the teacher would first incorporate an engaging hook that would conclude with stating the teaching idea. Next, the teacher would shift to the study of the text by including a transition statement that would introduce the book of Hebrews (stating for the listener the author's purpose, occasion for writing, and significant historical background). The background for Hebrews would conclude with the teacher setting the stage for the particular passage by providing the surrounding context and how the text fits within the scheme of the overall book.

After providing a hook, the teaching idea, and the background information of both the book and the passage, the teacher should write a lesson that includes one to three main teaching points, dividing the passage's verses according to each point. For example, the teaching idea identified above for Heb 4:14–16 breaks down easily into three points for the book portion of the lesson:

1. *Jesus is our great high priest (v. 14a, v. 15)*
2. *Holding fast to our confession (v. 14b)*
3. *Approaching God when in need (v. 16)*

After identifying the points of the passage and connecting each verse of the passage to a particular point, the teacher should flesh out exactly what will be taught under the corresponding point. An outline of this nature will provide clarity for the listener as well as highlighting the logical flow of a text. The best practice would be to write a verbatim manuscript, outlining what the teacher plans to say while teaching. This practice ensures that studied material from the inductive process is taught to the learner. For instance, the teacher may have questions that arose while she was "roaming" through the observation step. She may have found the answers to those questions during the interpretive step; and, if she had certain questions, those questions may have arisen for the listener as well. Thus, in reviewing her study notes, the teacher may craft the message in such a way as to raise a question for the listener from the text, which she then proceeds to explain for the learner.

For example, consider a question from Heb 4:14–16: What does it mean that we have a high priest who can sympathize with our weaknesses? And beyond that, what does it mean that Jesus was tempted as we are, yet without sin? The answers to both of those questions signify that the author of Hebrews was teaching rich theological truths about both the human nature and divine nature of Christ. In that one verse, one may conclude that Jesus is both God and man, for in Christ, believers have both a human high priest who sympathizes with us in our weaknesses (he understands what it is to be human) and a divine high priest who, while tempted in every way that we are, in his humanity never once sinned (he is sinless, because Jesus is the divine Son). Therefore, the teacher should plan to discuss each phrase of verse 15, explaining in detail how both the humanity and divinity of Christ display the perfection of Jesus as a great high priest.

Yet, the teacher would still have more to explain. From the observation and interpretation steps, she may have studied the institution and role of the high priest in Hebrew culture, reviewing how Old Testament books such as Leviticus delineate the functions of the priesthood. Further, the teacher might quickly reference particular Old Testament high priests. This particular background information could be taught under point one, so that listeners would be introduced to the need for a great high priest, contrasting Old Testament priests with Christ, who is the true and better high priest.

Look

While the "book" section's main goal is to teach the meaning of the text according to the author's intent for the original audience, the "look" section begins to push the teacher and learner to consider ways that the Bible passage applies to current day-to-day living. To prepare for this portion of the lesson, the teacher should reflect upon the work done in the inductive step of application. In chapter 7, several suggestions were given for ways to contemplate how particular passages could be applied, and each should be reviewed as the teacher crafts ways for the listener to "look" at her own life so that she might understand the timeless principle of the text. At the end of chapter 7, a three-step process articulated by Duvall and Hays was given that is helpful for writing the look section, specifically:

1. Observe how the principles in the text address the original situation.
2. Discover a parallel situation in a contemporary context.
3. Make your applications specific.[7]

---

[7] Duvall and Hays, *Grasping God's Word* (see chap. 7, n. 14), 244–47.

During the look portion of the lesson, the teacher may use the teaching time to discuss the parallel situation that listeners may encounter that corresponds to the Scripture. For example, consider 1 Corinthians 8, which concerns Paul's instruction to the church at Corinth about eating food sacrificed to idols in pagan temples in the city of Corinth. While believers today, for the most part in Western society, do not come from a cultural background that includes eating meat once offered to idols, the timeless principle of 1 Corinthians 8 has significant implications for Christians regarding how they love and interact with brothers and sisters in Christ. While the "book" portion on a lesson from 1 Corinthians 8 would explain the particular context of Paul's instruction regarding eating meat sacrificed to idols, the look portion might consider a similar situation that a modern Christian might face.

Thinking through a similar situation gets to the heart of the saying that a text has one meaning, but many applications. The meaning of 1 Corinthians 8, in context, was that a Corinthian Christian's freedom to eat meat sacrificed to idols should not take precedence over love for the weaker brother, whose conscience would have been "wounded" by such an act (1 Cor 8:12–13). The application for believers today would be to forego choosing their freedom for the sake of those who have a weaker conscience—for instance, a somewhat similar situation might exist between Christians who believe in a freedom to listen to secular music (that does not promote sinful thoughts or actions) and those Christians who believe that listening to any secular music is sinful (maybe due to their past life before meeting Christ). To apply the principle, then, would be for the believer who listens to secular music to forego that practice in the presence of the believer who finds secular music troublesome. The teacher, thus, uses the look portion of the lesson to make specific, contemporary applications derived from the meaning of the text. Or the Bible teacher may present a parallel situation in story form to the listeners, and then open this portion of the teaching event for small group discussion, which would allow for constructive conversation precisely designed to call listeners from passive engagement with the text to active assessment for personal implications. Such conversation will bring clarity for listeners, bridging the Bible's meaning from the book portion to allow everyone to look at how God's Word speaks to all of life, which then leads to obeying Scripture.

The "look" portion also offers a structured element for small group conversation. Classroom dialogue always risks getting off topic, so this section of the lesson should be carefully planned. The teacher should write out questions related to the book portion to be asked during the look section. Planning ahead in this way gives the teacher enough time to craft questions that will incorporate critical thinking for the small group, so each member can help the other, through discussion, consider ways to personally apply the text. Such questions, then, must not be ones simply answered by a yes or a no, but rather should be wh-questions (who, what, where, when, and how).

Took

In 1 Cor 1:28, the apostle Paul reminded the believers at Corinth that "we proclaim him, warning and teaching everyone with all wisdom, so that we may present everyone mature in Christ." The proclamation of Christ and teaching of the Scriptures have the effect of bringing immature believers into maturity in their walk with Christ. Such Christian maturity is demonstrated by obedience to Christ's commands, as Jesus himself taught that those who love him will keep his commands (John 14:15). The "took" portion of the outline, then, brings the teaching time to its logical conclusion by encouraging listeners to "be doers of the word and not hearers only" (Jas 1:22). As the teacher plans this last portion of the lesson, she may go back to the implementation step of the inductive method to draw upon insights gained on how to put the passage into practice. Thus, the lesson should conclude with the teacher pointing out specific, tangible ways to obey God's Word that are consistent with the main idea of the text. The nature of the audience must also shape the teacher's "took," and there are potentially two different types of attenders in the audience.

First, the teacher might consider that some listeners may not be followers of Christ. The teacher should always seek to incorporate the gospel into the lesson, and if the gospel has not been clearly stated, the teacher should explain the death, burial, resurrection, and ascension of Christ, defining sin and clearly articulating the need for repentance from sin and placing faith in the finished work of Jesus. Thus, the "took" for the unbeliever is a call to believe the gospel, explicitly conveying to unbelievers that apart from Christ, they do not have the capability of obeying the text. Second, for those who are in Christ, the "took" must be rooted in the gospel as well; believers should be reminded of the finished work of Christ and how the righteousness of Christ has been given to them through the work of the Holy Spirit. Therefore, the imperative commands stated within the text must be rooted in the work of Christ on their behalf, communicating that Christ ultimately has obeyed perfectly where they fail. When believers begin to understand the perfect righteousness of Christ, as well as how Christ's perfection has been credited to their account, they also will joyfully seek to obey the Scriptures knowing of their full acceptance on Christ's account. Teaching that is founded upon these theological truths then rescues learners from a moralistic, burden-inducing obligation to obey the Bible, translating the experience of obedience to a spirit-empowered, renewed heart that desires to honor and glorify Christ out of love for him and his commands.

Conclusion

This chapter outlines the use of the hook, book, look, took method for teaching the Bible. The five steps of inductive Bible study found in the first section may all be used to inform the crafting of a message, allowing for teachers to teach expositorily, while also creating opportunity for class dialogue once a text's meaning has been taught. For a template to use in writing out a teaching manuscript, see the appendix in this book.

9

The Life of the Teacher

May he make your hearts blameless in holiness before our
God and Father at the coming of our Lord Jesus with all
his saints. Amen. Additionally then, brothers and sisters,
we ask and encourage you in the Lord Jesus, that as you
have received instruction from us on how you should live
and please God—as you are doing—do this even more.
—1 Thessalonians 3:13–4:1

Teachers hold influence over those they teach. Ask anyone today about
a schoolteacher they had growing up, who had significant impact on
who they are as a person, and they will likely, with a smile and some nos-
talgia, be able to recount a story of the person who taught them and the
personal impact that person had on their life. Often, this type of influence goes beyond the subject that the teacher taught and extends to the
way the teacher interacted with their student, as well as the day-to-day
behavior they modeled in various life circumstances. The same type of
impact may be true of teachers in the church. Many believers can recount
mentors, disciplers, preachers, and teachers who influenced their beliefs
and walk with Christ—not by concepts they learned from the teacher—
but by watching and imitating their mentor's way of life. The Christian

teacher, then, must be committed to more than just proper hermeneutics and faithful exposition; they must also consider the way they live out what they teach. The apostle Paul teaches to this end when he notes that doctrine must be adorned with godly living (Titus 2:10) and thus he often exhorts his followers to imitate his way of life as he follows Christ (1 Cor 4:16; 11:1).

While learning the tools for properly teaching the Bible in its context is necessary for the ministry of teaching in the local church, the teacher herself will not be credible or trusted if she is not walking in holiness and exhibiting growth in godliness. Leaders in the body must exhibit certain characteristics of integrity if they serve publicly, for their way of life will either help or hinder the truths that they speak. The apostle Paul demonstrates this when he writes to Timothy regarding those who desire to be pastors. He mentions that these men should be:

> . . . above reproach, the husband of one wife, self-controlled, sensible, respectable, hospitable, able to teach, not an excessive drinker, not a bully but gentle, not quarrelsome, not greedy. He must manage his own household competently and have his children under control with all dignity. . . . He must not be a new convert, or he might become conceited and incur the same condemnation as the devil. Furthermore, he must have a good reputation among outsiders, so that he does not fall into disgrace and the devil's trap. (3:2–7)

While 1 Tim 3:2–7 concerns the qualifications to serve in the pastorate (not women who exercise their spiritual gift of teaching), an application from the text may be made. The idea is that if one desires to serve in ministry, one must meet basic qualities of godliness and integrity. These requirements highlight the necessity of pursuing holiness in one's walk, no matter the place of service in the local body. Additionally, every member of Christ's church is called to live a life that is pleasing to God. The New Testament epistles are replete with calls to honor God by one's lifestyle. Consider how the letters to the churches at Galatia, Ephesus, Philippi, and Colossae beckon every church member to pursue Christlikeness:

Now those who belong to Christ Jesus have crucified the flesh with its passions and desires. If we live by the Spirit, let us also keep in step with the Spirit. (Gal 5:24–25)

For you were once darkness, but now you are light in the Lord. Walk as children of light—for the fruit of the light consists of all goodness, righteousness, and truth—testing what is pleasing to the Lord. Don't participate in the fruitless works of darkness, but instead expose them. (Eph 5:8–11)

Therefore, my dear friends, just as you have always obeyed, so now, not only in my presence but even more in my absence, work out your own salvation with fear and trembling. For it is God who is working in you both to will and to work according to his good purpose. Do everything without grumbling and arguing, so that you may be blameless and pure, children of God who are faultless in a crooked and perverted generation, among whom you shine like stars in the world, by holding firm to the word of life. (Phil 2:12–16)

But now, put away all the following: anger, wrath, malice, slander, and filthy language from your mouth. Do not lie to one another, since you have put off the old self with its practices and have put on the new self. You are being renewed in knowledge according to the image of your Creator. (Col 3:8–10)

Each of the four Scripture references above provides just a few of the repeated calls in New Testament epistles to godly living. These texts highlight the ethics of Christian behavior and the means by which a godly life is accomplished—through the process of sanctification, wherein a believer "works out their own salvation" knowing that "it is God who is working" in them "according to his good purpose." In essence, the process of sanctification means that while the believer is made positionally holy at the moment of conversion, she must also pursue practical holiness by walking in step with the Spirit. This concept may appear confusing at first since Christians are imputed with the very righteousness of Christ.

If they are righteous in Jesus, why seek personal holiness? The answer is that one who has been truly born of God's Spirit will long for realized Christlikeness. They will mourn the sinful choices, thoughts, or habits that burden their lives, but will also long to see Christ formed in themselves. Think of Paul in Romans 7, who laments:

> For I know that nothing good lives in me, that is, in my flesh. For the desire to do what is good is with me, but there is no ability to do it. For I do not do the good that I want to do, but I practice the evil that I do not want to do. Now if I do what I do not want, I am no longer the one that does it, but it is the sin that lives in me. (Rom 7:18–20)

In Romans 7, Paul puts the experience of every true Christian into words: we desire to do good and delight in God's law, and yet, we feel as if we are at war with our flesh. Paul famously concludes Romans 7 with this statement: "What a wretched man I am! Who will rescue me from this body of death? Thanks be to God through Jesus Christ our Lord" (Rom 7:24–25a). Then, he goes on to announce that "therefore, there is now no condemnation for those in Christ Jesus, because the law of the Spirit of life in Christ Jesus has set you free from the law of sin and death" (Rom 8:1–2). This statement from Paul in Rom 8:1 and what follows in that chapter is truly the key to growth in Christ, to working out one's salvation and obeying all the imperatives for godly living, resulting in a life that matches what one teaches. The apostle sets up the tension believers live in by his comments in Romans 7, concluding that while Christians feel this sense of inability to please God in their flesh, the good news is that for those "in Christ" there is no more condemnation for sin. Christ has met all the righteous requirements of God's law, and God "condemned sin in the flesh by sending his own Son in the likeness of sinful flesh as a sin offering" (Rom 8:3).

This condemnation of Christ brings freedom for those who place their faith in Jesus. For Romans 8 teaches that God gave Christ as an offering for sin "in order that the law's requirement would be fulfilled in us who do not walk according to the flesh but according to the Spirit" (Rom 8:4). The chapter then begins to contrast what a fleshly mind versus a spirit-filled mind does: the mind focused on the flesh is set on or thinks upon fleshly things, is hostile to God, and does not submit to God; the mind set on the Spirit results in life and peace, and is marked by spiritual vitality. This concept is best summed up by Rom 8:5, "For those who live according to the flesh have their minds set on the things of the flesh, but those who live according to the Spirit have their minds set on the things of the Spirit." This verse relates to what Paul told the believers of Galatia: "I say, then, walk by the Spirit and you will certainly not carry out the desire of the flesh" (Gal 5:16). But how do we "walk by the Spirit"? How are we to live a life with our "minds set on the things of the Spirit"? The answer comes from how we actively engage with spiritual things in life, as Stott notes as he comments on the meaning of Rom 8:5:

> Now to "set the mind" (*phroneō*) on the desires of *sarx* [the flesh] or *pneuma* [the Spirit] is to make them the "absorbing objects of thought, interest, affection and purpose." It is a question of what preoccupies us, of the ambitions which drive us and the concerns which engross us, of how we spend our time and our energies, of what we concentrate on and give ourselves up to. All this is determined by who we are, whether we are still "in the flesh" or are now by new birth "in the Spirit."[1]

Stott's explanation of "having the mind set on the things of the Spirit" leads to a discussion on the inner life of the Bible teacher. What is it that "preoccupies" or drives us? What concerns take up most space in our mind? How do we spend our time and energy? What do we give our lives to? To ask these questions is to ask what we are setting our minds upon: the things of the flesh or the things of the Spirit? And if we find that we are setting our mind on the things of the Spirit, then surely, we will find ourselves walking by the Spirit, not carrying out the desires of the flesh. But how do we set our mind on the things of the Spirit, practically? Through the practice of spiritual disciplines.

---

[1] John Stott, *The Message of Romans* (Downers Grove, IL: IVP, 1994), 223.

Spiritual disciplines are practices we commit to as believers that help us to walk in communion with and obedience to the Lord Jesus. This chapter lists, defines, and discusses several spiritual disciplines. We will also consider the relationship between these disciplines and competency in teaching the Scriptures.

The Role of Spiritual Disciplines

Christians identify spiritual disciplines in various ways, but this chapter will focus upon four disciplines: 1) participating in the local church, 2) reading the Bible, 3) praying, and 4) singing psalms, hymns, and spiritual songs. Before we enter into a discussion of each spiritual discipline, all four practices must be rooted in a proper understanding of the role of spiritual disciplines. As mentioned above, spiritual disciplines are those practices that push us toward communion with and obedience to Jesus. Their function is to help us to abide in Christ and to obey Christ. As the previous section mentioned, spiritual disciplines help us to walk according to the Spirit, so that we do not fulfill the desires of the flesh. These practices engage us in the task of setting our mind on the things of the Spirit, or what could otherwise be called abiding in Christ, as Jesus taught about in John 15:1–8. In those eight verses, Jesus exhorts and/or mentions that his disciples are to "abide" in him, or as the Christian Standard Bible (CSB) translates the word, to "remain" in him multiple times, beginning with verse 4, which says, "Remain in me, and I in you. Just as a branch is unable to produce fruit by itself unless it remains on the vine, neither can you unless you remain in me." William Hendriksen explains that one's abiding in Christ is dependent upon Christ while paradoxically it is the responsibility of the believer:

> Hence, the words "Abide in me," do not constitute a condition which man must fulfill in his own power before Christ will do his part. Far from it. It is sovereign grace from start to finish, but *the responsibility of abiding in Christ is placed squarely upon man's shoulders, exactly where it belongs. Without exertion there is no salvation.* But the power to exert oneself and to persevere is

God-given! What is meant by abiding in Christ is explained in verses 7 and 9.[2]

Hendriksen's encouragement is twofold: abiding in Christ is accomplished only through the power of Christ, and Christians are to exert themselves in their efforts to abide in Christ. Abiding in Christ is passive, as the CSB hints at when it translates the word "abide" as "remain." Christians simply remain in Christ. However, remaining in Christ is not only passive but takes on an active nature. This active pursuit of abiding in Christ is explained, as Hendriksen noted, in verses 7 and 9:

> If you remain in me and my words remain in you, ask whatever you want and it will be done for you. (John 15:7)

> As the Father has loved me, I have also loved you. Remain in my love. If you keep my commands you will remain in my love, just as I have kept my Father's commands and remain in his love. (John 15:9–10)[3]

These verses teach that the art of abiding in Christ involves the Word of Christ remaining in the believer, as well as the Christian remaining in Christ's love by keeping Christ's commands. The role of spiritual disciplines is to aid in these endeavors: as we pursue participation in the local church, as we read the Bible, as we pray, and as we sing psalms, hymns, and spiritual songs, the Word of Christ will dwell in us and we will be compelled to obey Christ's commands, all through the divine empowerment of the Spirit.

Participating in the Local Church

To be a member of a New Testament church is to, at the simplest level, participate in listening to God's Word, partake of the Lord's Supper, fellowship with other believers, and pray. The pattern set forth in Acts 2:42

---

[2] Hendriksen, *New Testament Commentary: Exposition of the Gospel According to John*, vol. II (see chap. 5, n. 13), 299.

[3] Verse 10 included for context.

reveals this when it says of the early church: "They devoted themselves to the apostles' teaching, to the fellowship, to the breaking of bread, and to prayer" (Acts 2:42). Thus, when a Christian joins a faithful church, they are positioning themselves to abide in Christ through what the Reformers called "the means of grace" which are "certain resources that God has given us to help us grow in grace" and "they are called the 'means of grace,' because God actually works through them to sanctify us, to bring us to spiritual maturity. Through these, we learn to obey God, to live by faith, and to repent of sin."[4]

Consider how the Christian grows in a disciplined, godly life as they devote themselves to the apostles' teaching, fellowshipping with other Christians, taking the Lord's Supper, and praying with other believers. The main way the modern church commits itself to the teaching of the apostles is through the preached Word. Christian Bible teachers learn the Bible not only through personal study but also through listening to a preacher who has studied and exegetes a text consistently, week by week, year by year, book by book. A diet of the faithful exposition of God's Word communicates to the Christian sound doctrine and provides a foundation for personal study. Not only does the Christian grow through the preached Word, but also through fellowship with other believers. True Christian fellowship takes place as the covenant community comes together to hear God's Word and help one another apply and live out the truth of the Word together. But fellowship also takes place around the Lord's Table, as brothers and sisters remember the atoning sacrifice of Christ, in his broken body and shed blood, thereby consuming the bread and the cup as a means of proclaiming the gospel that unites them. When one shares in the Lord's Supper with other believers in the local church, they are often encouraged by pastors to assess themselves before partaking, seeking to repent of any known sin, and going to any brother or sister to pursue reconciliation (1 Cor 11:17–34). This practice highlights the care and concern spiritual leaders exhibit as they are charged to watch over the souls of their congregants. Thus, membership in the local church

---

[4] Frame, *A Theology of Lordship* (see introduction, n. 4), 918.

calls one to submit oneself to spiritual leaders as well as other believers (Heb 13:17; Eph 5:15–21), resulting in accountability to live a life worthy of the gospel. When faithful participation in a local church becomes a pattern for the Bible teacher, her life will exhibit the fruit of abiding in Christ, and she will be equipped for sound biblical teaching.

Reading the Bible

As discussed in chapter 1, the Bible is God's inspired, inerrant, infallible, authoritative, sufficient, necessary, and clear Word to mankind. Chapter 2 outlined the overarching story of the Bible as creation, fall, redemption, and restoration, while also pointing out that all of the Scriptures point to Jesus Christ. Chapter 3 reiterated that while the Bible contains 66 books written by 40 different authors over the span of 1,500 years, it presents God's story through the use of various genres that display the creative nature of God and of man, who penned the Scriptures under inspiration by the Holy Spirit. Because of these multiple characteristics of the Word, the Bible teacher must be devoted to a study of the Bible. God's Word is knowable but is also an intricate book that requires long-term, committed analysis. The best place to begin with a study of the Bible is to read it—all of it. This exhortation may sound simplistic, yet some struggle with a desire to read the Bible in its entirety; others may have the desire but struggle with follow-through after making such a commitment. For the person who believes they have been given a spiritual gift of teaching, who lacks a desire to dig deeply into the Bible, to study it in-depth with all of its nuances, help from God should be sought. Over and over again, the psalmist prays in Psalm 119 about loving God's law. Bible teachers ought to add the prayers of Psalm 119 to their own daily prayer and will surely find that God answers the prayer of the one asking to grow in love for and understanding of his Word.

Beyond praying for God's help, two types of reading plans are suggested for daily reading, which help not only the person who struggles with a desire to read the Bible but also the one who lacks discipline in their commitment. Readers may find it beneficial to use an app or website that allows them to check off their reading for either of the following plans. The two suggested reading plans are the Robert Murray M'Cheyne Plan and the Chronological Bible Plan, which are both accessible on apps/websites such as ESV.org, the ESV app, biblegateway.com, the Bible Gateway app, or the YouVersion app. Choosing one of the plans and committing to reading the assigned daily Scriptures for each plan may take the average reader around 20–30 minutes a day. Consistently reading through the Bible year after year will enhance the Bible teacher's ability to understand particular passages when seeking to exegete a text for a lesson because over time she will see how one text relates to the whole. Both the M'Cheyne and the Chronological Plans are exceptional at revealing Scriptures's interconnectedness, thus it is suggested that the plans be alternated from year to year.

The Robert Murray M'Cheyne Plan breaks the entire Bible down into four readings per day, with both Old and New Testament texts. Readers can expect to read through the Psalms and the New Testament twice in a year with this plan. One of the most beneficial aspects to reading through M'Cheyne's plan is that you will begin to discern how passages are connected to one another, causing you to grow in your understanding of the unity of the Bible, the divine authorship of the Bible, as well as how Scripture may be used to interpret Scripture. For example, recently while reading through this plan, on October 4, the assigned passages included: 1 Kings 7, Ephesians 4, Ezekiel 37, and Psalms 87–88. One powerful connection may be seen in comparing the events of Ezekiel 37 with a few verses from Psalm 88. Ezekiel 37 concerns the vision God gives Ezekiel about the valley of dry bones. When God brings Ezekiel to this valley, he tells him:

> "Son of man, these bones are the whole house of Israel. Look how they say, 'Our bones are dried up, and our hope has perished; we are cut off.' Therefore, prophesy and say to them, 'This is what the Lord God says: I am going to open your graves and bring you up from them, my people, and lead you into the land of Israel. You will know that I am the Lord, my people, when I open your graves and bring you up from them." (Ezek 37:11–13)

This wonderful picture of resurrection power became even more clear when reading from one of the daily psalms, which says:

> Do you work wonders for the dead?
> Do departed spirits rise up to praise you? *Selah*
> Will your faithful love be declared in the grave,
> your faithfulness in Abaddon?
> Will your wonders be known in the darkness
> or your righteousness in the land of oblivion? (Ps 88:10–12)

The questions posed by the psalmist—"Do you work wonders for the dead? Do departed spirits rise up to praise you?" are some of a few hints at the resurrection in the Old Testament, with Ezekiel 37 bringing an even fuller picture into view. After reading Ezekiel 37 and reflecting upon the four questions of Ps 88:10–12, we are left to proclaim a resounding, "yes!" This provides one of the many wonderful examples of the joy that may be experienced by reading through the Bible using the Robert Murray M'Cheyne Plan.

The Chronological Reading Plan offers a unique perspective for those who are unfamiliar with the biblical story. Often, Old Testament history can be very confusing for those who have not taken a survey course that explains the details of the storyline and of God's people, Israel. One might feel like they are stumbling around in the dark, for example, when reading prophetic books, like the book of Ezekiel mentioned above, if they have not come to understand the entire biblical plotline, as it unfolds chronologically through time. Bibles are arranged with the Old Testament books being listed according to category: the books of the Law (the first five books), history (Joshua–Esther), poetry (Job–Song of Songs), major prophets, and minor prophets. Since the books are organized in this manner, the reader does not fully grasp the connection between the historical books and the prophetic books; yet, reading through a chronological plan allows the reader to see the direct relationship or the historical background to particular prophetic passages.

For instance, in the Chronological Plan, the reading for July 8 is 2 Kings 15 and 2 Chronicles 26, both of which speak about the reign of King Uzziah (also known as King Azariah). The reading for the following day, July 9, is Isaiah 1–4, which mentions King Uzziah: "The vision concerning Judah and Jerusalem that Isaiah son of Amoz saw during the reigns of Kings Uzziah, Jotham, Ahaz, and Hezekiah of Judah" (Isa 1:1). Since the reader would have been reading through 2 Kings and 2 Chronicles, and then is sent to read in Isaiah, they are given the timeline of events as it happened in Israel and Judah chronologically. Yet two days later, they will read in Amos and will also read from Micah within the same few days. Reading the Bible in this way will bring clarity to the Bible teacher as she comes to know the story as it unfolds rather than relying upon commentaries to fill in the missing pieces.

Praying

In Ephesians 6, the apostle Paul exhorts the church to "Pray at all times in the Spirit with every prayer and request, and stay alert with all perseverance and intercession for all the saints" (v. 18). The admonition to pray at all times in the Spirit comes at the end of the section on the armor of God, as it reminds the believer that they are engaged in a spiritual battle, where they must "stay alert with all perseverance." This truth reminds the Christian of that moment of battle in the life of the Lord Jesus, as he charges the disciples in the garden of Gethsemane on the night of his betrayal: "Stay awake and pray, so that you won't enter into temptation. The spirit is willing, but the flesh is weak" (Matt 26:41). Additionally, the writer of Hebrews encourages believers by calling them to pray: "Let us approach the throne of grace with boldness, so that we may receive mercy and find grace to help us in time of need" (Heb 4:16). Thus, the Bible teacher must recognize the necessity of prayer in the life of the Christ-follower. The teacher must be in prayer during those times when she studies God's Word, but more than that, she must view communion with God through prayer as an essential component of her Christian life. Donald Whitney underscores this thought in his book *Spiritual Disciplines for the Christian Life*, when he quotes Martin Luther, who once said, "As it is the business of tailors to make clothes and of cobblers to mend shoes, so it is the business of Christians to pray."[5]

It could be argued that Martin Luther understood the necessity of prayer as a Christian leader, because he certainly was aware of the battle Christians face in the realm of spiritual warfare. Having penned the famous words of the Reformation hymn, "A Mighty Fortress Is Our God," Luther calls upon the Christian to remember that "still our ancient foe doth seek to work us woe, his craft and power are great, and armed with cruel hate," yet he calls the believer through those lyrics to remember that strength alone comes from Jesus, who is on our side in the midst of battle. Thus, we rely upon Christ, in whom we stand, and who is himself praying for us, interceding on our behalf. With this in mind, you may be encouraged to follow Luther's explanation of using the Lord's Prayer as the model for daily prayer (which may be found on several different websites). Another resource for incorporating prayer into one's daily life as a pattern would be to pray through a psalm a day, meditating upon the psalmist's words, speaking them back to God, and pouring them out with heartfelt, personal words that come to mind in the moment. Praying God's Word will bring insight to the meaning of Scripture in a fresh way, anchoring the words of the Bible into the soul of the believer.

Singing Psalms, Hymns, and Spiritual Songs

Singing is not normally listed as a spiritual discipline, but if we are to pray the psalms, then surely we should also remember that they were given as a means of worship through song. New Testament believers were exhorted to continue the same practice of singing, specifically in the book of Colossians. Paul instructs the church: "Let the word of Christ dwell richly among you, in all wisdom teaching and admonishing one another through psalms, hymns, and spiritual songs, singing to God with gratitude in your hearts" (Col 3:16). As we seek to learn God's Word and meditate upon it, this verse cannot be missed, for in it we learn that

---

[5] Donald Whitney, *Spiritual Disciplines for the Christian Life* (Colorado Springs: NavPress, 1991), 68.

through music—psalms, hymns, and spiritual songs—the word of Christ dwells in us richly, and when we sing these songs, teaching and admonishing take place. Surely then, this verse indicates that spiritual growth happens when we enjoin our hearts to praise God through worshipful, truth-filled songs. Some of the most encouraging, instructive means of personal growth can take place for Christians, who listen to others' own struggles and their faith in God and his promises, accompanied with music. A few recommended resources are four live albums that contain glorious hymns and spiritual songs produced by Sovereign Grace Music: *Together for the Gospel Live*, *Live II*, *Live III*, and *Live IV*.

Conclusion

This chapter sought to outline four spiritual disciplines: participating in the local church, reading the Bible, praying, and singing psalms, hymns, and spiritual songs. These four habits are some of the most fundamental means of growing in Christlikeness for any believer. Thus, these practices are essential for those who would desire to be found faithful when handling God's Word. One cannot be thoroughly equipped to teach the Bible without first giving one's life to it. Being formed by the Word in the local church, reading it, praying it, and singing it will lay the strong foundation needed for understanding and applying the Bible personally and teaching it to others.

10

Doctrinal Teaching

> Not many should become teachers, my brothers, because
> you know that we will receive a stricter judgment.
> —James 3:1

In the introduction, "Why Women Should Teach the Bible," readers were asked to consider the Great Commission and how Jesus's words applied to both men and women—how both genders are commanded by Christ to go and make disciples, baptizing them in the name of the Father, the Son, and the Holy Spirit, teaching them to observe all that Christ commanded. The introduction explored what the phrase "teach them to observe all that I have commanded" means, and concluded that Jesus was instructing his disciples to pass on his teachings, a body of doctrine. While the pastors/elders of the church have been given the responsibility to shepherd churches through biblical teaching and protecting doctrine, each church member must know true doctrine, have the ability to discern false doctrine, and teach sound doctrine to others. We see this truth implicitly when Jude begins his epistle: "Dear friends, although I was eager to write you about the salvation we share, I found it necessary to write, appealing to you to contend for the faith that was delivered to the saints once for all" (Jude 1:3). The recipients of Jude's letter were being called upon "to contend for the faith," which Thomas Schreiner points out as a "focus on the gospel rather than the detailed doctrinal formulas of later church history. And yet we must also acknowledge that the gospel itself involves doctrines that must be confessed. We have an early recognition here that the touchstone for the Christian faith is in the teaching of the apostles and that any deviation from their teaching is unorthodox."[1] Thus, Bible teachers must concern themselves with orthodox biblical truth—they must know theology.

But what is theology? While many would simply define theology as "the study of God," could it be more than study? Is it not what Ephesians 4 is teaching—a knowledge of God's Son, not for mere knowledge, but that results in something: unity in the faith and maturity into the fullness of Christ? Thus, theology could be better defined as "knowing God and being formed into the image of Christ."[2] This definition presses us to go beyond the traditional definition of theology—of simply knowing about God. As Thornton notes, "the reason for defining theology this way is because the Bible does not paint theological knowledge as an academic study or a set of correct beliefs or thoughts, but more so a dynamic growth experience of both *knowing* (God) and *changing* (into the image of Christ)."[3] Consequently, the Bible teacher must understand the commitment to doctrinal teaching begins and ends with a desire for a true knowledge of God amongst those she teaches resulting in the transformation of the listener into Christlikeness. And the content which she teaches should be consistent with orthodox doctrine, in an effort to encourage listeners to know God and grow in his likeness.

But what are the doctrines that make up the core teachings of the church? In recent years, Christians have been quick to name someone as a heretic or to identify something taught as heresy with little to no

---

[1] Schreiner, *New American Commentary: 1, 2 Peter, Jude* (see chap. 1, n. 13), 436.

[2] Christy Thornton, "Theological Study," in Kristin L. Kellen and Julia B. Higgins, *The Whole Woman: Ministering to Her Heart, Soul, Mind, and Strength* (Nashville: B&H, 2021), 145.

[3] Thornton, 145.

understanding of how to determine that which constitutes actual heresy. Because of this, the concept of "theological triage" helps one to determine those doctrines that are central to the Christian faith, allowing the Bible teacher to identify particular teachings that should be taught with care and precision. "Theological triage" is a term that was first introduced by Albert Mohler in a 2005 article entitled, "A Call for Theological Triage and a Call for Christian Maturity." In the article, Mohler relates the medical practice of triage (where doctors and nurses determine whom to treat in an emergency situation according to the seriousness or weightiness of injury) to the need for Christian leaders to triage or classify items of first-rank or order. He writes, "I would suggest three different levels of theological urgency, each corresponding to a set of issues and theological priorities found in current doctrinal debates."[4] Those items he lists as first-level are: "the Trinity, the full deity and humanity of Jesus Christ, justification by faith, and the authority of Scripture."[5] Thus, this chapter seeks to provide help to the Christian teacher who, on the one hand loves teaching the Bible, but who, on the other hand, has never considered the weightiness of teaching God's truth. James 3:1 hints at the idea of stewardship in teaching when it says, "Not many should become teachers, my brothers, because you know that we will receive a stricter judgment." The task of teaching the Scriptures brings with it a very serious warning: those who do so will be judged strictly. Therefore, we should determine to understand doctrines of the faith, so that we are equipped to teach well. This chapter seeks to outline core doctrines and how to integrate doctrine into one's teaching, as well as pointing out common false doctrines that are outside of orthodox Christian belief. Finally, the chapter calls for a personal commitment to one's own church's doctrinal beliefs while not teaching in contradiction to its stated beliefs.

---

[4] R. Albert Mohler Jr., "A Call for Theological Triage and a Call for Christian Maturity," July 12, 2005, https://albertmohler.com/2005/07/12/a-call -for-theological-triage-and-christian-maturity.

[5] Mohler Jr., "A Call for Theological Triage."

Core Doctrines

Popular practice in sermon and lesson development today includes pointing the preacher or teacher to discerning the theological implications of a passage so that they can point such implications out for the listener. But what if one does not have a background in studying basic theological categories or dogmatics?[6] How can they discern the theological implications of a passage if they are mostly unaware of the various doctrines of the faith or of how to articulate such doctrines in a biblically faithful manner? For instance, one may believe in the Trinity, but may not have studied this doctrine in enough depth to understand the intricacies of Trinitarianism, and the ways that this doctrine has been explained throughout church history. This section, then, seeks to offer a broad overview of the core doctrines of Theology Proper, Christology, and Soteriology for the Bible teacher.

Theology Proper

Christopher Morgan and Robert Peterson define Theology Proper as "the study of the doctrine of God, including the Trinity, God's attributes, and works."[7] A discussion of such topics can quickly lead into what might feel like an academic exercise. Yet, readers should be encouraged that when we talk about God, who he is, and what he does, what we are doing is entering into that which we will be doing for all eternity: learning more and more about our triune God, and, in the words of John Piper, glorifying him by enjoying him forever. Thus, this section should lead one to great joy in our great God. To briefly lay a foundation for the core doctrine of Trinity, let's consider a definition:

> . . . almighty God's eternal existence in three persons: Father, Son, and Holy Spirit. The Father is the first person of the Trinity, the Son the Second Person, and the Spirit the Third Person. These

---

[6] Dogmatics is defined as "of or relating to dogma (doctrine or a set of doctrines)." See Hernando, *Dictionary of Hermeneutics* (see chap. 1, n. 21).

[7] Christopher W. Morgan and Robert A. Peterson, *A Concise Dictionary of Theological Terms* (Nashville: B&H Academic, 2020), 164.

three persons are one God and are inseparable, sharing the same essence. We distinguish the persons from one another but do not confuse them. We thus hold that only the Son of God became a man and died for our sins. Each person is fully God, and mysteriously, the three divine persons indwell one another (this is called perichoresis). Although in unity they share all of their works, they perform specific tasks. To cite an example, Scripture attributes the source of redemption to the Father (in election), its accomplishment to the Son (in his death and resurrection), and its application to the Spirit (in regeneration and conversion).[8]

This definition highlights how we understand the Trinity correctly. We should teach in a way that does not undermine the Godhead as one God, existing in three persons who share the same essence. The definition also relates that we are to distinguish the persons of the Godhead from one another and that we are not to confuse them. A common way of differentiating the three persons is to say something to the effect that the Father is not the Son and the Son is not the Spirit. Additionally, biblical language teaches us how the Trinity eternally relates to one another: the Father begets the Son and the Son is begotten of the Father (John 3:16 KJV) and the Holy Spirit proceeds from the Father and the Son (John 15:26). This language is what theologians term the "eternal relations of origin" which is the only way the persons of the Trinity are differentiated—thus, the mind and the will of the Trinity is one and unified. All of these truths fall under the term "ontological Trinity," helping us to understand *who God is*. But what about *what God does*? To answer this question, another term is employed: "economic Trinity" which "concerns the roles that the Father, Son, and Holy Spirit play in creation, and especially in salvation. The Father sends the Son to rescue the lost, the Son performs the work of redemption, and the Spirit applies salvation to believers."[9]

Thinking through these terms may not feel as if knowing them really applies to the ministry of teaching. Consider how thinking this way may

---

[8] Morgan and Peterson, *A Concise Dictionary of Theological Terms*, 165.
[9] Morgan and Peterson, 166.

well lead to inadvertent heresy. A common illustration used to describe the differences in the Trinity is the water metaphor. In this illustration, it is commonly said that the Trinity is like water, as water exists in three forms: gas (steam), liquid, and solid (ice). All are water, different in form, but water cannot be steam, liquid, and ice at the same time. This example illustrates a misunderstanding or ignorance about the Trinity, and in reality is a heresy known as Modalism (or Sabellianism) which states "that the three persons were divine successively, not simultaneously. The one God revealed himself first as Father, then as Son, and finally as Holy Spirit."[10] This teaching is fleshed out, for instance, when one teaches that while Jesus was on earth, God the Father and God the Spirit were not in existence. This teaching directly violates passages such as John 16 and 17, where Jesus tells the disciples he is going to the Father (John 16:5), that he will send the helper, the Holy Spirit (John 16:8), and also when we witness Jesus praying directly to the Father: "When Jesus had spoken these words, he lifted up his eyes to heaven, and said, 'Father, the hour has come; glorify your Son that the Son may glorify you'" (John 17:1). Each of these passages clearly reveals that the Son is not the Father, the Father is not the Son, and the Spirit is not the Son nor the Father—the Trinity exists in three persons, who are one God.

Another error of note regarding Theology Proper concerns a denial of one of God's attributes, mainly that he is omniscient (all-knowing), while also attacking God's sovereignty and providence. This view, called Open Theism, is defined as the "view that God neither controls nor knows the future; also called openness theology, the open view of God, or free will theism. . . . Open theism is a serious error, for, according to Scripture, God controls (Pss 33:10–11; 135:6; 139:16; Dan 4:34–35) and knows the future (Isa 42:8–9; 44:6–7; 46:9–10)."[11] Those who hold to this view seek to emphasize man's free will and God's accommodation of himself to allow for human choice that is not predetermined.

This section outlined a proper definition of the Trinity and provided two Trinitarian terms (ontological and economic) to lay a foundation for

---

[10] Morgan and Peterson, 166.
[11] Morgan and Peterson, 127.

precise care when one teaches about the Godhead. Two heretical views were then presented: Modalism and Open Theism. Each of these views is related to Theology Proper. The next section considers Christology and will offer common heretical teachings on the person and work of Christ.

Christology

While the previous section covered items related to the Godhead in general, this section is devoted to those teachings that concern the incarnate Son of God in particular. The need for understanding basic Christology does not only benefit one's teaching ministry, but is helpful for personal edification and growth as one comes to understand the identity and natures of the incarnate Son. Further, the truths of Christology actually undergird the gospel itself. The question that must be considered, then, is *who is Jesus?* Christology seeks to answer that question by teaching us that Jesus is fully God *and* fully man. John 1 and Colossians 1 both help us to understand the two natures of Jesus:

> In the beginning was the Word, and the Word was with God, and the Word was God. He was with God in the beginning. All things were created through him, and apart from him not one thing was created that has been created. (John 1:1–3)

> The Word became flesh and dwelt among us. We observed his glory, the glory as the one and only Son from the Father, full of grace and truth. (v. 14)

> He is the image of the invisible God, the firstborn over all creation. For everything was created by him, in heaven and on earth, the visible and the invisible, whether thrones or dominions or rulers or authorities—all things have been created through him and for him. He is before all things, and by him all things hold together. He is also the head of the body, the church; he is the beginning, the firstborn from the dead, so that he might come to have first place in everything. For God was pleased to have all his fullness dwell in him, and through him to reconcile everything to

himself, whether things on earth or things in heaven, by making peace through his blood, shed on the cross. (Col 1:15–20)

These Scriptures relate to us both the divine and human natures of the Son of God. The key to remember is that Jesus is one person (the Son of God) with two natures (and his two natures are inseparable and unconfused). These truths are essential to the gospel itself, as Robbie F. Castleman notes, "Christology matters because in Jesus, God took on our flesh through the virgin's womb; lived in our flesh through his life, baptism, temptation, and sinful community; suffered in our flesh through dying and death; proved the reality of our redemption's fullness in his resurrection; and recapitulated our humanity in his ascension."[12]

The question of who Jesus is was a considerable conversation in the years following the early church, as various church fathers discussed Christ's nature and his work. In the midst of these conversations, significant heresies arose:

- Arianism—Taught that Jesus is a created being, is not eternal or divine
- Apollinarianism—Believed that Jesus had a human body and soul, and only a divine mind;
- Nestorianism—Emphasized that there are two separate persons dwelling in Jesus "to the point of dividing his person"[13]—Christ the man, and Logos the divine; results in a denial of the unity of the God-man
- Eutychianism—Taught that Jesus's nature was a mix of human and divine; denies that in Christ there are two separate natures

Simply put, these errors are teaching that either Jesus is not God (Arianism), Jesus is a mixture of humanity and divinity (Eutychianism), Jesus's body and soul were not divine, only his mind was (Apollinarianism),

---

[12] Robbie F. Castleman, "On Christology," in *Themelios* 29, no. 1, accessed January 16, 2022, https://www.thegospelcoalition.org/themelios/article/on -christology/.

[13] Morgan and Peterson, *A Concise Dictionary of Theological Terms*, 30.

or Jesus is divided into two separate people (Nestorianism). Thus, texts like Heb 1:3 are helpful at this point: "The Son is the radiance of God's glory and the exact expression of his nature, sustaining all things by his powerful word. After making purification for sins, he sat down at the right hand of the Majesty on high" (Heb 1:3). This verse reveals to us that Jesus is of the same essence as God; it teaches that Jesus is God, in addition to Scriptures like John 1, which speaks of the Word becoming flesh and dwelling among us. Yet, the human nature of Christ is also exemplified throughout the Gospels as Jesus, in his humanity, eats, sleeps, grows in wisdom and stature, etc. Thus, the four heresies listed above illustrate the type of false teachings the Council at Chalcedon was seeking to combat, which resulted in the articulation of the Definition of Chalcedon "which outlines Orthodox Christology . . . [and] explicitly rejects each of the major Christological heresies":[14]

> Following the holy fathers we confess one and the same our Lord Jesus Christ, and all teach as one that the same is perfect in Godhead, the same perfect in manhood; truly God and truly man; the same of a reasonable soul and body; consubstantial with the Father in Godhead and the same consubstantial with us in manhood; like us in all things except sin; begotten before the ages of the Father in Godhead; the same one in these last days, and for our salvation, born of Mary the Virgin Theotokos [Godbearer] in the manhood; one and the same Christ, Son, Lord, unique; recognized in two natures, unconfusedly, unchangeably, indivisibly, inseparably; the difference of natures being by no means taken away because of the union, but rather the distinctive character of each nature being preserved, combining in one person and hypostasis; not divided or separated into two persons, but one and the same Son and Only Begotten God, Word, Lord Jesus Christ; as the prophets of old, and the Lord Jesus Christ himself,

---

[14] Steven A. McKinion, "Jesus Christ," in *Historical Theology for the Church*, ed. Jason G. Duesing and Nathan A. Finn (Nashville: B&H, 2021), 33.

have taught us in his regard, and as the creed of the fathers has handed down to us.

Notice the clarity this definition brings about Christ. It affirms that Jesus is Lord, that he is God and man, that he is consubstantial (of the same essence) with the Father and with us as man, that he is like us in all things minus sin, that he is begotten of the Father, that he was born of a virgin, and that he has two natures that are united in one person. All of these affirmations find their basis in the Scriptures. The Virgin Birth is predicted in Isa 7:14, coming to fruition in two of the four Gospels (Matt 1:18–25; Luke 1:34–35). John 1:1–5, 14 teaches that the eternal Son was with God in the beginning and that the Son became flesh. John 3:16 tells of the begotten-ness of the Son, while Phil 2:6–11 indicates that Jesus existed as God but in a moment in time "assumed the form of a servant, taking on the likeness of humanity" and came "as a man." The Christ-hymn of Philippians also teaches that Jesus is and will be exalted as Lord. This statement or definition from Chalcedon, which itself articulates biblical concepts concerning the person of Jesus, helps one to discern when teachings about Christ's divinity or humanity are incorrect.

While this is not an exhaustive list of the heresies concerning Christ, each of these errors demonstrates confused teaching about the person of Christ as it relates to his divinity and humanity. Bible teachers should be aware of such confusion and continue to study the Bible for precise language that will cause one to consider their own personal beliefs, and what they have been taught about the divinity and humanity of Jesus. Ultimately, clarity on the person of Christ brings clarity on how one teaches the gospel. For example, if one were to teach a confused view of the two natures of Christ—possibly emphasizing the humanity of Christ without clearly articulating the divinity of Christ—the gospel would not make sense. Christ is able to save his people because he is fully God and fully man.

Soteriology/Anthropology

One last serious error to be explored is that of Pelagianism, which presents both an unbiblical view of man (biblical anthropology) and the doctrine of salvation (soteriology). Pelagianism concerns the teachings of Pelagius, who believed that "human nature retained a permanent capacity for sinlessness, which in turn influenced will and action" and thus advocated that human beings were not fallen in Adam's sin—that they did not inherit a sin nature from Adam (thus they were not born in sin, also known as "original sin").[15] Consequently, Pelagius taught that man could live righteously apart from the grace of God, invalidating the need for a salvific work of Christ on sinner's behalf. He was a moralist who posited that Adam was a bad example and that Jesus is merely a good example. Yet, from the previous section, we know that Jesus, being God, took on flesh to live as man—not to provide an example of a godly life but to live the godly life that we cannot. Thus, the gospel teaches us that we don't need an example; we need a Savior and that salvation is a gift of God bringing justification for sin through the perfect, sinless Son and his death, burial, resurrection, and ascension.

But how might some teach Pelagianism today? This view relates to those who would teach that a person may be saved based upon their good works, otherwise known as "works-based righteousness." The Bible, however, teaches that man is fallen and has inherited a sin nature from his father, Adam, but needs an atoning sacrifice for sin, which is all of grace (Rom 5:12–21; Eph 2:1–10).

Equipped to Teach Sound Doctrine

This chapter sought to present a few of the false doctrines that have plagued the church throughout history, in an effort to better prepare Bible teachers. One helpful reminder is that spiritual growth and understanding in doctrine is a process accomplished by the work of the Holy Spirit in the life of the believer. While Bible teachers should feel the weight and seriousness of teaching that accords with "the faith once for all delivered to the saints," they should also remember that there is room for growth in learning sound doctrine and the ways to properly articulate

---

[15] Coleman M. Ford, "Salvation," in *Historical Theology for the Church*, 104.

it. Therefore, readers should commit to the process: learn doctrine, grow in theological knowledge, but do so to honor God and for edification (of self and others). God will be honored when his Word and doctrine are correctly taught, but believers will also be encouraged by a deepening knowledge of who God is and what he has done in the world through the work of his Son and the Spirit.

This call to know God and to mature in him is the very essence of why teachers have been given as a gift to the church. Ephesians 4:11–15 teaches this concept:

> And he himself gave some to be apostles, some prophets, some evangelists, some pastors and teachers, to equip the saints for the work of ministry, to build up the body of Christ, until we all reach unity in the faith and in the knowledge of God's Son, growing into maturity with a stature measured by Christ's fullness. Then we will no longer be little children, tossed by the waves and blown around by every wind of teaching, by human cunning with cleverness in the techniques of deceit. But speaking the truth in love, let us grow in every way into him who is the head—Christ.

This text shows that Jesus himself gave various gifts of grace (see Eph 4:8) to the church; verses 11–15 reveal those gifts and their purpose. The "gifts" are the apostles, prophets, evangelists, pastors, and teachers, who are all leaders for the church who specifically engage in the ministry of teaching. Therefore, the purpose of these gifts, or leaders of Christ's church, were called with a goal in mind—that Christ's body be built up to reach unity and maturity. This unity consists of agreement in faith and in knowledge in the person of God's Son, so that the church might mature and grow into the fullness of Christ. Once this growth in maturity into Christ has taken place, these verses teach that the church will no longer fall prey to "every wind of teaching" or, in other words, the body will no longer be like little children, going from one teaching to the next. John Stott comments about these "little children" that Paul mentions, indicating that they "are immature Christians. They never seem to know their own mind or come to settled convictions. Instead, their opinions tend to be those of the last preacher they heard or the last book they read, and they fall an easy prey to each new theological fad."[16] As Christians are taught by church leaders, they grow in doctrinal understanding and are equipped to do the work of the ministry (Eph 4:12).

These verses in Ephesians specifically point to the gift of those who serve and lead the churches, for instance the God-called, God-ordained elders/preachers that the churches learn from, week in and week out. Yet, the person who teaches or disciples others in God's Word, who is not called to be an elder, whether they are male or female, should long for a unity based upon faith in Christ and knowledge of Christ so that those they mentor and teach mature in Jesus. Thus, while every member is not called to the pastorate, they are called to maturity and growth in Christ, and helping others with the same. Ephesians 4:15 shows this, for it follows that when we grow into maturity and are no longer "tossed by the waves and blown around by every wind of teaching" that the members of Christ's body will be about the task of "speaking the truth in love." That is why *every* member should cultivate a love of theology in their hearts and minds. However, since this book is written with women in mind, remember that the apostle Paul himself advocated for women to learn during a time when it would have been unpopular culturally to do so, for he wrote to Timothy, "A woman is to learn quietly with full submission" (1 Tim 2:11). This verse, to some, may sound offensive, however, the truth is meant to be encouraging:

> It is important to observe that the sole imperative in this verse is the command to learn. In Paul's day, this was the countercultural element that would have stood out: women are obliged to learn the word of God every bit as much as men, despite regular Jewish prohibitions against teaching women Torah.[17]

---

[16] John Stott, *The Message of Ephesians* (Downers Grove, IL: InterVarsity, 1979), 170.

[17] Craig L. Blomberg, "Women in Ministry: A Complementarian Perspective," in *Two Views on Women in Ministry*, ed. James R. Beck (Grand Rapids: Zondervan, 2005), 167. Blomberg goes on to explain the verse: "*Hēsychia* does not mean 'silence'. . . . The cognate adjective *hēsychios* has appeared as

Women are to learn the faith and teach the faith. Like every church member, they do so with the understanding that the elders are those specifically appointed by God to oversee the church, to teach, instruct, and protect doctrine (Acts 20:28; 1 Pet 5:1–4; 1 Tim 5:17). Thus, one should regard pastors/elders as the leaders giving oversight in the area of the church's stated beliefs, and church members ought to teach in ways that support, not contradict, the official articles of beliefs of their local church. One place to begin, then, in understanding all the doctrines of the faith would be to acquire one's faith statement from their local church. The Bible teacher should review the doctrinal beliefs that the church has posted for their members, to become better acquainted with the way the church has articulated its position on core doctrines of the faith. Not only should female Bible teachers learn these doctrinal beliefs, but she should also desire to teach and mentor other women to know and love theology, so that "speaking the truth in love, [all would] grow in every way into him who is the head—Christ" (Eph 4:15).

---

recently as in 2:2 to refer to the kind of lives all believers are to live—"peaceful and *quiet*," cooperative and caring, *not* never speaking! *Hypotagē* is cognate to the verb for 'submission' (*hypotassomai*) in 1 Corinthians 14:34 and suggests some form of subordination. Again, this is behavior for students, male or female, that is always appropriate, even though what is considered submissive or cooperative may vary from one culture to the next."

11

Contexts for Teaching Women God's Word

> In the same way, older women are to be reverent in behavior,
> not slanderers, not slaves to excessive drinking. They are to
> teach what is good, so that they may encourage the young
> women to love their husbands and to love their children, to be
> self-controlled, pure, workers at home, kind, and in submission
> to their husbands, so that God's word will not be slandered.
> —Titus 2:3–5

What are the ways women are involved in teaching the Bible in evangelical churches today? The answer depends upon a variety of questions and their answers. Does that church have a stated position on gender roles? For instance, does the church hold to egalitarianism (which believes in the equality of men and women, and no distinction of roles) or complementarianism (which believes in the equal dignity, value, and worth of men and women, but believes in differing roles in the church and the home)? If the church is egalitarian, then the practice for that type of church would be that women exercise teaching gifts in any context, including serving as an elder who preaches from the pulpit. It would follow then, that in egalitarian churches, women who are not in the position of teaching elder but do have the gift of teaching would be involved in other teaching contexts beyond the pulpit in that local body, with no restriction.

If the church is complementarian in nature, however, different questions arise about the ways women are involved in teaching in the local church. For complementarian churches, the question must be asked: Where does its practice fall within the spectrum of beliefs on men and women, and their role within the church? While this book is written from the complementarian perspective (holding that the office of pastor/elder is open to only qualified men, and men are responsible as the head of the home), it must be understood that complementarians do not all agree on how to apply their complementarianism. Those who hold to complementarianism interpret the exercise of teaching gifts in a wide variety of ways, and particular interpretations of complementarianism influence and determine the various contexts in differing churches for women to teach the Bible. For example, on one end of the complementarian spectrum, women are only permitted to teach the Bible through informal, female-to-female discipleship relationships, while on the other end of the spectrum, one might believe that in the church "anything that an unordained man is allowed to do, a woman is also allowed to do."[1]

Yet, a church's stance on the application of complementarianism is not the only element to consider when discussing contexts for women to teach the Bible. Another aspect of the church's ecclesiology that must be discerned is its view of discipleship and the role of Bible study in the formation of disciples. Every church's strategy for Bible study is different: some prefer a traditional Sunday school model, while others seek to incorporate small groups. Some opt for weekly accountability discussions that are less driven by Bible study, and others organize groups for a discussion on how to apply the pastor's Sunday sermon. Other churches offer core classes that contain a lecture-based style on topics related to the faith and are typically offered within a semester. Various churches employ various methods, and sometimes they offer a blend or mix of all the types mentioned so far. Additionally, while some churches may or

---

[1] Kathy Keller, *Jesus, Justice, & Gender Roles: A Case for Gender Roles in Ministry* (Grand Rapids: Zondervan, 2012), 21.

may not offer formal small groups or have a Sunday school ministry, they often incorporate a teaching time for children and youth that is fashioned after an old-school Sunday school model. With all these modes of Christian education in the church, it is critical that ministry to women be considered especially in complementarian churches that do not offer direct avenues for women to teach the Bible (whether in a space like a traditional Sunday school class or in women's Bible studies).

The question, then, for these type of churches, is two-fold: How do women exercise their teaching gifts and how is Bible study incorporated into the life of believers, so that disciples are being formed? This chapter seeks to discuss the contexts where female Bible teachers may exercise their teaching gifts and how they can be equipped to disciple women through various programming in the local church in the area of ministry to women: special events and Bible studies. Types of teaching will be considered while thinking through inductive Bible study, lesson preparation, and teaching the text expositionally.

Teaching the Bible in a Local Church Women's Ministry

Many churches have either a formal women's ministry with a women's ministry director or a team of volunteers who make up a committee that facilitates the church's ministry to women's programs. Often, these women lead the women's ministries in at least three ways: they plan and execute special events (such as retreats or conferences), they facilitate mentoring relationships amongst the women, and they organize Bible studies (which are often offered in the fall and the spring). Women's ministry leaders should evaluate their ministries to see how the Bible is specifically incorporated into each of these three areas since the particular method of Bible incorporation communicates something to the women of the church.

An evaluation is needed because women's ministry events are simply not what they could be. Over the past decade, leading evangelical women have used their voice, through writing and speaking, to lament the stereotypical women's ministry and call for a higher bar to be set. For example, Wendy Alsup wrote a blog in 2009 entitled, "Pink Fluffy Bunny

Women's Bible Studies" and her comments from that blog resonate with many women of the faith. Alsup writes,

> There is a lot of emotional fluff out there masquerading as Bible study—stuff that quotes chick flicks and romance novels more than it does Scripture. Then there are some Bible studies that quote Scripture, but they don't deal with Scripture in context. They just pick and choose the verses that support their topical agenda. And that gets on my nerves as well. Even among the more conservative, reformed authors, the books tend to be singularly focused on the topic of women's roles. Where are the simple, focused Bible studies?[2]

What Alsup was assessing in 2009 became a larger conversation in the years that followed, so much so that Jen Wilkin, in a 2017 article for *Christianity Today*, posited that "women's ministry is undergoing a renaissance."[3] That article included a link to an episode from *The Calling* podcast where Wilkin offered her evaluation: "Women's ministry is at a pivotal moment. I think that it will either take the old model and 'Pinterest it up' so that it looks new—or it will begin to see itself as an arm of the church that is uniquely positioned to equip women for the work of discipleship." Wilkin makes an excellent point: women's ministry can be a vital component in the local church for developing female disciples. Yet, ministry leaders must recognize its value and potential, and they must cast a vision for this area of the church to be a vital means of discipleship of women.

---

[2] Wendy Alsup is a published author, having written books such as *Practical Theology for Women* (2008) and *Is the Bible Good for Women?* (2017). She previously served as a deacon of women's theology and teaching at Mars Hill Church. This quote comes from her blog post, "Pink Fluffy Bunny Women's Bible Studies," December 4, 2009, https://theologyforwomen.org/2009/12/pink-fluffy-bunny -womens-bible-studies.html.

[3] *Christianity Today*, "Jen Wilkin: Let's Make This a Golden Age for Women's Ministry," *The Calling* Podcast, March 8, 2017, https://www.christianitytoday .com/ct/podcasts/calling/jen-wilkin-lets-make-this-golden-age-for-womens -ministry.html.

Often a women's ministry is driven by events rather than a vision for discipleship. These events include special events and Bible studies that do not necessarily lead women to a deeper study of God's Word. In the first chapter ("The Nature of the Bible") and in the second chapter ("The Overarching Story of the Bible"), we considered the wonderful ways God speaks and reveals himself through special revelation (that is the Bible, God's story of the redemption of mankind), we come to know Jesus, are reconciled through the gospel, and are being conformed into the image of God's Son. One must be equipped to study and teach God's Word for knowing God and growing in Christlikeness. Thus, in the chapters that followed, inductive Bible study was introduced, so that Bible teachers might be better equipped to develop expository lessons. The purpose of doing expository lessons helps both the teacher and the learner, since it draws them into a method of discerning the true meaning of Bible texts, increasing wisdom and understanding in God's Word. When a woman stands and teaches the Bible in this manner, the women who watch and hear another woman who is capable of discerning and articulating the meaning of the Bible hopefully will be enlightened to the idea that she, too, should take seriously the study of the Scriptures. The women's ministry is the avenue to facilitate this type of teaching for the women of the church and can be accomplished through special events and Bible studies.

Special Events

Throughout the years, the popular model for women's ministry has included hosting a conference, retreat, or special event at the church. These special events in the past have looked like ladies teas, craft nights, or some other similar get-together, and more than likely include a special guest speaker. Retreats and conferences are sure to include a guest speaker or speakers, and often a theme Bible verse is chosen for these events. Speakers might be given one or more sessions, with an allotted time period for each session, and may even be given an assigned topic that relates to the theme. Bible teachers should commit to teach the assigned topic by choosing Bible texts that relate to the topic, yet the text itself should not be molded to fit what the speaker wants to say or to the theme. The Scripture should always be taught in a manner that reflects the authorial intent of a passage, not simply as a proof-text for the conference theme. She should seek to walk the audience through the text, verse-by-verse. Sometimes, Bible teachers may state that they believe in expository teaching, but in practice, still do not teach according to the point of the passage. They may read the text, state an idea from the text, and jump to application points, teaching the Bible in a way where they emphasize the way the Scripture relates to present-day life without first outlining what the Scripture meant in its original context. Thus, the teaching may feel more like the Bible was mentioned and moral lessons and stories were conveyed rather than giving insight into the meaning of the words, phrases, and concepts the biblical writer sought to convey for an original audience. This type of Bible teaching can leave the listener not feeling nourished by the Word and does not form the listener in doctrine and deep teaching for sanctification.

Additionally, if a Bible teacher is contacted and asked to teach at a local church where she does not attend, it might be helpful to have one or more discussions with church leadership (the pastor of discipleship, the women's ministry leaders[s], etc.) to determine the topics that would benefit the women generally in their growth in discipleship. As mentioned before, often women's ministry events focus on topics related to being a wife or mother, or deal with areas such as marriage, parenting, friendship, and mentoring. While these are beneficial topics to teach on, leaders might think about subjects related to the Christian faith that will provide a strong foundation for women in theology. The Bible teacher might suggest conference themes related to topics in the areas of biblical theology or Theology Proper (God's attributes, the person and work of Christ, The Trinity). If the Bible teacher will be speaking at a church that is not her own, she might also peruse the church's website to determine that particular body's doctrinal standards, making sure to teach in accordance with the church's stated beliefs.

As female leaders in the church serve women through special events, especially if they are tasked by the church to develop female disciples, leaders may consider incorporating scope and sequence, which will help leaders to think through what disciples need to know and how to identify appropriate curriculum. Doing so will bring better clarity to how events are planned—the events will be driven by the vision and goals of the ministry, rather than planned without thought of how the event will shape women in their walk with Christ.[4]

Bible Studies

Typically, women's ministry programs in the local church rely upon outside sources to provide Bible studies. These studies are purchased from a publisher, and often include videos of a Bible teacher explaining the text(s), along with workbooks that have daily assignments for women to complete. Sometimes, these workbooks do not incorporate higher level thinking and keep the learner in the lower realms of learning (elements such as recalling and restating). Bible book studies also sometimes include lots of stories illustrating present-day circumstances, with a few questions about various verses from the Bible book being studied. These questions are short answer and fill in the blank, which might be an okay place to begin for a new believer, but most of these types of Bible study do not demonstrate how to understand books of the Bible in their context, and how to engage in higher level thinking (analyzing, evaluating, and applying within proper context to the point of the text). Thus, women in the church who have been given a spiritual gift of teaching for the edification of the church might seek to rely less on published Bible studies, and model inductive Bible study by teaching exegetically, training women to study their Bibles in the same way.

This leads to an additional element that should be incorporated into the women's ministry program: leadership development in the area of Bible teaching. What does this look like practically? Consider how the areas above (special events and Bible study curriculum) often draw upon outside teaching of women. Planned special events might bring

---

[4] For those interested in a discussion on the discipleship process of the local church, two books are recommended: *Deep Discipleship: How the Church Can Make Whole Disciples of Jesus* by J. T. English and *Discipleship Essentials: A Guide to Building Your Life in Christ* by Greg Ogden.

in a speaker who is not related to the church but is popular in larger groups related to women's ministry. Bible studies are chosen because of a writer's platform within the world of evangelicalism. Women in the churches definitely learn and grow from leaders outside of their body, yet leaders might evaluate if there has been an over-reliance upon outside teachers through special events and Bible studies. The church might consider what it would look like for women in their local body, who feel gifted in teaching, to acquire proper training (from pastors or seminary classes, or through books such as this one). Identifying those women and equipping them to teach might then bear the fruit of creating church-specific Bible studies (with the topics chosen in mind of those particular women in a particular local body, and the areas where they need to grow in doctrine and biblical literacy). The result might be weekly events hosted and led by women in the church, rather than relying upon teaching from outside sources.

While some churches have women's ministries that plan special events and Bible studies for women, another component of church ministry related to teaching the Bible is that of small groups or Sunday school. The difference between small groups and Sunday school is goal oriented: in many churches, small groups lean toward the goal of fellowship, while Sunday school leans toward the goal of Scripture knowledge. If a church has small groups, but does not have Sunday school, female leaders should consider leveraging a women's ministry for women to study and teach the Bible. If a church has Sunday school, leaders should contemplate offering at least some gender-specific classes (if they do not already offer them) where women have the ability to learn and grow from other women who are proficient in teaching the Scriptures. And for those women who are involved in churches where curriculum is provided for a small group or Sunday school environment, they ought to think through the design of the curriculum and if the curriculum itself integrates expository teaching—meaning the curriculum should be assessed to see if it helps the learner understand the background to the Bible book, teaches the context, and identifies the main point of a passage. If a teacher finds herself with assigned curriculum that does not accomplish these tasks well, she should be able to study in such a way that she supplements the curriculum with her own study of the text.

The end of the matter is this: women should be given a context where they can teach the Word in the local church. Why? Because Christ's church will grow and others will be discipled in the faith. This issue requires active leadership among women's ministry leaders and pastors alike. Do you know of a space for women to teach God's Word? If not, how can you become an advocate for helping the church understand where it might be lacking?

CONCLUSION

It is one thing to say that women are permitted
to teach women, and quite another to deliberately cultivate
and celebrate their teaching gifts.
—Jen Wilkin[1]

I love the quote from Jen Wilkin above. It gets to the heart of this book's message: empowering and equipping women to teach by actively cultivating the teaching gifts of women in the church. This text is a means to teach women why they should be teaching the Bible and how to do it, and was broken into two parts: principles and practice.

In the introduction, we considered several biblical reasons for why women should be taught to teach. This may seem odd to some—that an apologetic for female Bible teaching was necessary. Yet, the current landscape of church culture over the past twenty years begs for a gentle correction to elements that have prevented women from exercising their teaching gifts. These elements include a change from small groups to Sunday school, along with a misunderstanding of biblical texts and a misapplication of complementarian theology. Thus, the introduction laid a solid foundation from the Bible for women to be equipped to teach. We considered first of all that both genders have been commissioned by the resurrected

---

[1] Jen Wilkin, "The Complementarian Woman: Permitted or Pursued?" April 23, 2013, https://www.jenwilkin.net/blog/2013/04/the-complementarian-woman-permitted-or.html.

Christ to "go and make disciples of all nations, teaching them to observe" all that Jesus commanded. If women are to be about the work of the Great Commission, this includes both announcing the gospel to the lost and discipling the converted to understand the doctrines of Jesus. We also considered a particular pattern for teaching in the local church from Titus 1 and 2, where elders are appointed to oversee the local church, and that they must hold to a body of doctrine so the church is built up with sound doctrine and is able to refute false teaching. This leads to the gender-based discipleship that the apostle Paul outlines in Titus 2, calling for women to "teach what is good." From there, we discussed the empowerment of the Holy Spirit, as he gives gifts of grace that are not based upon gender to every member of a local church for the church's edification, and these gifts include speaking and teaching. Finally, in the introduction, we discovered a few descriptive examples of New Testament women who taught the Scriptures in the midst of the various circumstances of their lives.

As the introduction laid the foundation for women teaching, chapter 1 laid the foundation for teaching the Bible. Why should we be concerned with teaching the Scriptures? Because they make up a part of the very revelation of God himself to us. We considered how creation displays God to us generally and how the Word of God reveals God specifically. Readers were challenged to consider their "doctrine of the Word" so that they might adopt an attitude of dependence upon Scripture so they teach not according to any authority in their own right but so others they disciple might understand the authority of the Bible. From there, the book covered the overarching story of the Bible in chapter 2, outlining the four key markers that reveal the major theme of the Bible, which are creation, fall, redemption, and restoration. This chapter also highlighted Jesus Christ as the main subject of the Bible and related ways that a Bible teacher might connect every passage to the gospel and to Christ. In chapter 3, the various genres of the Bible were introduced, underscoring the creativity of God as he used various human authors and different types of literature to convey his message to his people: narrative, law, poetry, prophecy, the Gospels, epistles, and apocalyptic books.

Chapter 4 defined the concept of hermeneutics and relayed an introductory history of evangelical interpretation, along with identifying current methods of interpretation. Chapter 5 introduced the inductive Bible study method as a means for studying a text to discern the author's intended meaning. Inductive Bible study begins with observing a text, and the suggested method of observation is to "ROAM" through the Scripture by reading, observing, asking questions, and meditating. Chapter 6 delved further into the inductive Bible study method by considering how students might interpret the Scriptures (by getting to the "MEATT" of a passage) and generalize the passage (by stating the exegetical idea in one sentence and translating that idea into a teaching idea). Chapter 7 introduced ways that Bible teachers can apply the Bible personally (and help students to do the same) as well as implement the Bible (seeking to go beyond personal application to obeying the Bible). This concluded the first section on principles.

The second section covered various ways to put into practice what was discovered in the first section. Chapter 8 suggested using the "hook, book, look, took" method crafted by Richards and Bredfeldt in their book, *Creative Bible Teaching*. This simple outline is a memorable device for constructing a message based upon an exegeted text of Scripture. Chapter 9 centered more around the practice of godliness, where Bible teachers were encouraged in the spiritual disciplines that might increase their knowledge and love for God's Word, which in turn increases their effectiveness in teaching. Chapter 10 sought to introduce the reader to basic theological categories, thinking through ways the teacher might be aware of doctrine, preventing false teaching. Chapter 11 concluded the book with ways female leaders might think through contexts for teaching women the Bible in the local church, especially through a women's ministry.

Thus, this book hopes to enlighten women to mainly two ideas: they should be involved in teaching the Scriptures, and they should know how to do it well—they should be equipped to teach. Wilkin's quote above points to a great need: how to deliberately identify, equip, grow, and encourage one gender to pursue how God has gifted them for the edification of the church through teaching. Other evangelical women have been encouraging the church to consider her stance on the gifts of women over the last decade. This call for women to be teachers of the Word arises from a place of care and concern for over half of the body, so that the church might grow in love for God and his Word, passing it along to others, so that they too might go and make disciples of all nations to the end that Christ's commands are observed. Consider this final question a charge—to women in leadership and to the pastors who shepherd them—in your context, what would it look like for you to empower and equip women to teach?

APPENDIX:
TEACHING MANUSCRIPT TEMPLATE

Passage:

Passage Subject:

Passage Complement:

Exegetical Idea:

Teaching Idea:

Body of the Lesson

Hook:

Propositional Statement (Teaching Idea):

Book Background (Context, author, historical setting, occasion for writing, etc.):

Book:

Point 1.   Verse(s):

Your Plan to Explain the Text:

Illustration:

Point 2.   Verse(s):

Your Plan to Explain the Text:

Illustration:

Point 3.   Verse(s):

Your Plan to Explain the Text:

Illustration:

Look:

Description of the parallel situation:

Discussion questions for the group:

Took (A measurable out-of-class assignment):

Conclusion (Restate teaching idea and 3 points):

NAME & SUBJECT INDEX

SCRIPTURE INDEX